Buy To Let Tax Planning

Lee J Hadnum

IMPORTANT LEGAL NOTICES:

WealthProtectionReportTM
TAX GUIDE - "Buy To Let Tax Planning"

Published by:
WealthProtectionReport.co.uk
Email: sales@wealthprotectionreport.co.uk

First Edition: February 2014

Copyright

Trademarks

DISCLAIMER

1. Please note that this tax guide is intended as general guidance only for individual readers and does NOT constitute accountancy, tax, legal, investment or other professional advice. WealthProtectionReport and the author accept no responsibility or liability for loss which may arise from reliance on information contained in this tax guide.

2. Please note that tax legislation, the law and practices by government and regulatory authorities (for example, HM Revenue and Customs) are constantly changing and the information contained in this tax guide is only correct as at the date of publication. We therefore recommend that for accountancy, tax, investment or other professional advice, you consult a suitably qualified accountant, tax specialist, independent financial adviser, or other professional adviser. Please also note that your personal circumstances may vary from the general examples given in this tax guide and your professional adviser will be able to give specific advice based on your personal circumstances.

3. This tax guide covers UK taxation mainly and any references to 'tax' or 'taxation' in this tax guide, unless the contrary is expressly stated, are to UK taxation only. Please note that references to the 'UK' do not include the Channel Islands or the Isle of Man. Addressing all foreign tax implications is beyond the scope of this tax guide.

4. Whilst in an effort to be helpful, this tax guide may refer to general guidance on matters other than UK taxation, WealthProtectionReport and the author are not experts in these matters and do not accept any responsibility or liability for loss which may arise from reliance on such information contained in this tax guide.

CONTENTS

ABOUT THE AUTHOR

Lee Hadnum LLB ACA CTA is a UK tax specialist. He is a Chartered Accountant and Chartered Tax Adviser and is the Editor of the popular tax planning website:

www.wealthprotectionreport.co.uk

Email Lee directly at:

Lee@wealthprotectionreport.co.uk with tax planning questions.

Members of www.wealthprotectionreport.co.uk can access thousands of articles and free tax planning books.

Lee is also the author of a number of best selling tax planning books including:

- **Tax Planning Techniques Of The Rich & Famous** - Essential reading for anyone who wants to use the same tax planning techniques as the most successful Entrepreneurs, large corporations and celebrities

- **The Worlds Best Tax Havens** – 220 page book looking at the worlds best offshore jurisdictions in detail

- **Non Resident & Offshore Tax Planning** – Offshore tax planning for UK residents or anyone looking to purchase UK property or trade in the UK. A comprehensive guide.

- **Tax Planning With Offshore Companies & Trusts: The A-Z Guide** - Detailed analysis of when and how you can use offshore companies and trusts to reduce your UK taxes

- **Tax Planning For Company Owners** – How company owners can reduce income tax, corporation tax and NICs

- **How To Avoid CGT In 2013/2014** – Tax planning for anyone looking to reduce UK capital gains tax

- **Buy To Let Tax Planning** – How property investors can reduce income tax, CGT and inheritance tax

- **Asset Protection Handbook** – Looks at strategies to ringfence your assets in today's increasing litigious climate

- **Working Overseas Guide** – Comprehensive analysis of how you can save tax when working overseas

- **Double Tax Treaty Planning** – How you can use double tax treaties to reduce UK taxes

1. REDUCING INCOME TAX ON INVESTMENT PROPERTY

You'll be subject to income tax on rental income from your buy to let properties at your marginal rate of income tax. This means that if you're a higher rate taxpayer you'll pay income tax at 40% (rising to 45% if your income is above £150,000). Any deductions you can make will therefore directly save tax at 40% for a higher rate taxpayer.

We'll have a look below at some of the main income tax deductions that owners of buy to lets should be considering:

Accountancy and legal fees

Allowable legal and professional costs that may be claimed include:

- costs of obtaining a valuation for insurance purposes,
- the normal accountancy expenses incurred in preparing rental business accounts and agreeing tax liabilities,
- the costs of evicting an unsatisfactory tenant in order to re-let the property.

Interest

This is likely to be one of the largest tax deductions and we've devoted an entire chapter to this.

Travelling Expenses

If you could get a full deduction for the costs of your visits to and from your property that could represent a very nice tax deduction. Not surprisingly though, the taxman looks to restrict this deduction as much as he can.

The fundamental rule when looking at claiming a deduction for any expenses is that it must be incurred 'wholly and exclusively' for the purposes of the buy to let business.

So the costs of travelling between different properties solely for the purposes of the rental business are an allowable deduction in computing rental profits but the initial cost of travelling from your home to the buy to let property and back will only be allowable if the purpose is entirely a business one.

Advertising

Costs of any advertising you incur will be allowable. This will apply whether the advertising is online or offline. So a joining fee for a property lettings website to advertise your property will be allowable.

Bank Fees

Any bank fees you incur in the letting will be deductible.

Removal Expenses

The costs that you may incur in transporting any furniture to the buy to let property would be deductible.

Training Courses

If you attend one of the many 'How to make a fortune in the property investment market' courses, ensure you claim that as a deduction.

Associations/Subscriptions

If you join property rental associations any subscription fee will be allowable.

Bad Debt

You can claim a tax deduction for any bad debts.

Insurance

Costs of insurance would be allowable

Pre 'Trading' Expenditure

When assessing your deductible expenses, remember that you can claim a tax deduction for expenses incurred up to seven years prior to the start of the trade. So if you incurred any allowable expenses when you were setting up the letting -- make sure you claim for them.

Repairs

These are always allowable for any rental or trading business. The key point here is to distinguish between 'revenue' expenses and 'capital' expenditure. Only the first of these can be offset against your rental income, as the latter is treated as part of your base cost for capital gains tax purposes.

The broad distinction is that repairs involve placing an asset into the condition that it originally was, whereas capital expenditure involves improving it in some way. Having said, that a cost normally remains revenue expenditure where any improvement arises only because you use new materials that are broadly equivalent to the old materials. A good example here would be replacing old lead pipes with new copper ones.

Examples of common repairs that are normally deductible in computing rental business profits include:

- exterior and interior painting and decorating,
- stone cleaning,
- mending broken windows, doors, furniture and machinery such as cookers or lifts,

- re-pointing, and
- replacing roof slates, flashing and gutters.

Salaries

If you wanted to you could employ a friend or relative to assist in your running of the buy to let business. This may be the case particularly where you have more than one property.

You'd be looking to claim any salary paid to them as a tax deductible expense of your rental business. The fact that the employee is a close relative or friend does not prevent the deduction. However it's crucial that there are genuine services provided by the employee in return for the salary. If there is no non-business purpose to the remuneration and the salary is not determined by the relationship you, it should be allowable.

You should therefore look for any salary paid to be at a market rate for the services provided.

Gardening

Payments to a gardener for garden maintenance would be deductible

Local Rates/Council Tax

Any local property taxes or similar expenses will be allowed as a deduction when calculating your rental profits.

So, there you have it. When you've calculated the rental profits, you simply include these on the land & property pages of the tax return, and pay tax at your marginal rate of income tax.

If there was a rental loss this would be ringfenced for tax purposes and could just be offset against other UK rental profits (either of the current year or future years).

2. MAXIMISING TAX RELIEF FOR INTEREST

If you own a buy to let property minimizing income tax on the rental income will no doubt be a key issue. Given the highest income tax rate is at 45% this can represent a significant reduction in your take home profits.

One of the main tax deductions will be your tax deduction for interest.

The tax legislation states that you'll obtain a tax deduction for any interest you incur 'wholly & exclusively' for the purposes of the lettings business. So in the straightforward scenario where you have a purchase of a buy to let property with a buy to let mortgage, the interest on the mortgage will clearly be allowed as a tax deduction as it's used 100% for the purposes of the lettings business.

The same rule will apply if you already own the buy to let propert and you take out another loan which is used to do up or renovat the buy to let property. Again in this case the loan is used solel for the use of the buy to let property.

Multiple properties

If you have more than one buy to let property this is treated as rental business for tax purposes. This means that once a rent business has started, all activities will be treated as carried out i the course of one business.

Any later expenditure leading up to the letting of the second ar later properties is part of the rental business and can be deducte So once you've got the first property up and running any futu loans for any properties would be deducted from the rent business profits as a whole (even for example if the seco property was not actually let yet).

Source doesn't matter

Another key point to bear in mind is that the source of any debt doesn't matter. As the Revenue manuals state:

'...The security for borrowed funds does not determine the use of those funds.

It is very common in small businesses for loans to be secured on the proprietor's home, because that is the only substantial owned asset. This is not relevant to the consideration of the use of the funds borrowed. Similarly guarantees given by another person do not affect the use of the funds...'

So you could have debt secured over your main residence which would qualify for interest relief if the funds were used for the rental business.

Wider application of the rule for capital withdrawals

In fact though the rules go much wider than just applying if the debt was used 'wholly & exclusively' for the purposes of the letting.

You could, for example, have a case where an individual owned a property as a main residence. This may be valued at £200,000. They may want to purchase a new property for themselves to live in, and rent out their existing main residence.

In this case they could remortgage the existing property to £100,000 and use this to finance a purchase on the new main residence they were to occupy. Would the interest on the £100,000 qualify for relief? You would think not based on the 'wholly & exclusively' requirement as its clearly been used to purchase a private residence.

In fact though interest on the £100,000 could qualify for relief.

The Revenue state that business owners (including buy to let landlords) are entitled to withdraw their capital from the business, even though substitute funding then has to be provided by interest bearing loans. In the example above it could be regarded as funding the transfer of the property to the business at its open market value.

So they'd argue that the wholly & exclusively requirement is still being met.

Whether debt is raised on a main residence to purchase a BTL (clearly allowable for interest relief) or whether debt is raised on the current BTL which is then used to purchase a main residence the capital account is the same. In the latter case they're extracting cash from the business. The fact that it needs to be replaced with interest bearing debt doesn't impact on the fact that the interest is incurred wholly & exclusively for the purposes of the business.

Note that the position is completely different if the capital account is overdrawn. In other words you can't be classed as extracting your capital from the business as there is no capital left. In this case if you took on debt which was extracted you'd be classed as extracting the debt -- and if it wasn't used for business purposes the interest would not then be deductible.

This could be the case if you've already taken significant value ou of the rental business.

Any debt?

The above looks at debt secured on the property (ie mortgag debt). What about other forms of debt - is that also allowable?

In theory it should also apply to other debts. Providing there i sufficient capital in the business the interest bearing debt replacing the funds that have been withdrawn from the rent business.

3. CALCULATING YOUR INTEREST DEDUCTION WHEN THERE IS AN OVERDRAWN CAPITAL ACCOUNT

As we've seen in the previous chapter the general rule is that you are entitled to a tax deduction for any interest that you incur 'wholly & exclusively' for the purposes of the rental business.

So in the straightforward scenario where you borrow money to buy a buy to let property, the interest on that loan will be completely allowable for income tax purposes.

It doesn't matter whether the loan is secured over the buy to let property or over your main residence - it will still be allowable providing the funds are used to purchase the property.

What about the converse position - where you have a buy to let property and you borrow money secured against it to use for your own private purposes?

You'd think it wouldn't be allowable - as it's not used for the purposes of the business, but this isn't necessarily the case.

Your rental property is classed as a rental business (just like any other kind of business). For tax purposes you're entitled to the same tax deductions as a trader may have.

The rules state that you're allowed to extract profits and even capital from the business if you wish. This is essentially just taking out the profits and equity. If you then need to inject cash via a loan to cover the cash you've taken out that's still viewed as a business purpose (ie providing working capital for the business).

So if you bought a property for £100,000 and had a £80,000 loan you'd have a capital account of £20,000.

The business may generate profits of £20,000 so you'd have a £40,000 capital account.

You could, if you wanted to, increase the mortgage to £100,000 and extract the cash. The interest on the additional debt should still be allowable as its just funding (and covered by) the business assets.

So you can extract cash from a rental business which is financed by debt without there being a reduction in the interest deduction.

Where the Revenue do draw the line though is where you have an overdrawn capital account with the business.

It's not straightforward and you would essentially need to look at the accounts and assess:

(1) Whether the net assets of the business were negative (ie net liabilities)
(2) The extent to which private drawings have caused the ne liabilities, and
(3) Whether this was financed by by bank debt.

Note though that as revaluations are treated as an unrealised cash flow for this purpose you'd not take into account any revalue property level. On this basis the assets of the business may b overdrawn if you had substantial debt and had remortgage numerous times to take account of increasing property prices.

If there were net liabilities you'd then need to look at the cause c the net liabilities. To the extent that it was caused by spending th realised cash on further rental properties it shouldn't result in a interest restriction. The jist of the guidance in the HMRC manua seems to focus on where the bank debt finances private drawings.

Example

So if you had the following:

A bought a BTL for £100,000 in 2001. He had a mortgage of £95,000. He therefore had a capital account of £5,000. He made rental profits of £20,000.

He took a loan from the bank of £50,000 and extracted £40,000.

His capital account is overdrawn by £25,000 in this case (ie £5,000 equity + £20,000 profits less than £50,000 loan).

If he extracted £40,000 of drawings this is financed by the £5,000 equity, the £20,000 profits and then £15,000 of the loan.

In this case 15,000/50,000 of the interest on the loan would not be deductible for income tax purpose.

Losses and Depreciation

As well as revaluations you also need to look at other adjustments that may need to be made when calculating the extent to which the interest is deductible.

Any losses may reduce the capital account but would not reduce the interest deduction (given it's effectively a business expense). Depreciation also artificially reduces the profits and would need to be ignored for this purpose.

For example, if in the example above A had realised a loss of £20,000 after £5,000 depreciation his capital account would be overdrawn by £60,000. Of this £50,000 debt, £15K went to finance the £15K losses, leaving £35K. He extracted £40K which was represented part by the £5K equity. Therefore 35/50 of the loan is not allowable.

These type of calculations are made where capital accounts are overdrawn and although potentially complex should be looked at globally (ie a general view should be taken).

4. JOINTLY HELD PROPERTY AND INCOME TAX

Married couples often own property and other investments jointly. This is an area that is potentially ripe for tax planning particularly where one spouse is a higher rate taxpayer and the other isn't.

In this case it's certainly worthwhile considering adjusting the ownership percentages to make full use of a spouse's personal allowance and basic rate income tax band. This is pretty common tax planning and transferring assets to a lower earning spouse can see rental income or bank interest taxed at 20% as opposed to 40%. But how in practice should the transfer be undertaken?

The first option is to actually amend the legal/beneficial title and transfer an interest to your wife. Therefore in the case of property this could be shown to be owned 75% by a husband and 25% by a wife to ensure the wife was taxed on 75% of the rental income.

This is a perfectly acceptable transaction and married couples do not have to hold assets in joint names. They can hold them separately; and they can divide up joint assets so that they hold them separately for the future. Each spouse is then taxed on the income from the assets each holds in his or her own name.

HMRC would have no objection to the division of joint assets where this is done genuinely. The only caveat here is that there may be problems where a division takes place but one spouse retains some sort of interest in an asset which is held in the other's name. In such a situation the settlements legislation may apply and deem the income arising to belong to the original owner of the asset.

Therefore if you still retained an interest in the income from a bank account that you transferred to your wife you could be assessed on 50% of the income. This could be the case if for example, t income was passed to you after it was credited to your wife's account.

As well as actually transferring property legally into different ownership proportions, an alternative is to retain the property in joint ownership.

The standard rule is that investment income from jointly held property is split equally between each spouse for tax purposes; however, where the true split is different a couple can opt to be taxed on that basis.

Therefore by making a declaration that the ownership of an asset is in fact different, it is possible to reallocate taxable income and the underlying ownership of assets between a married couple. The declaration would be made on a form 17 available from HMRC.

Note that a married couple don't have a general option to have income taxed in any way they like. You can depart from the standard 50:50 split for tax purposes where:

•each spouse is in fact entitled to a share other than 50:50 in the property and
•the share that a spouse has in the income is the same as their share in the property

The declaration on form 17 sets out the beneficial ownership percentages and would ensure that each spouse was taxed on that basis. You could therefore own a bank account jointly but allow 99% of the income to be taxed on your wife. Note however, in the case of a bank account you would need to change your ownership from 'joint beneficial owners' eg by way of a deed.

Once a declaration is made it remains in force until your interests in the capital or income change. Note however, that the form is not retrospective and can only apply to income that arises from the date the declaration/form is signed, so make sure if you plan to use it that you send it in ASAP.

5. WEAR & TEAR ALLOWANCE AND CAPITAL ALLOWANCES

Anyone who lets residential property has two key options when it comes to claiming relief for capital expenditure incurred on let property.

They can:

- Claim the wear and tear allowance
- Claim capital allowances

In this chapter we look at the tax impact of these different options.

Wear and tear allowance

A wear and tear allowance is given as a deduction for 10% of the 'net rent' from furnished lettings. This is intended to cover the depreciation of plant and machinery, such as furniture, fridges etc supplied with the accommodation which could otherwise not be eligible for a tax deduction.

In order to calculate the wear and tear allowance you simply take 10% of the net rent received. (The 'net rent' is based on the rent you obtain less any charges and services that would normally be borne by a tenant but are borne by you as the landlord such as council tax or water rates).

The 10% deduction is intended to cover the sort of assets that tenant would usually provide in unfurnished accommodation. This includes general household items such as:

- Beds
- Sofas
- TV's

•Fridges and white goods
•Carpets
•Curtains
•Utensils etc

As well as claiming the wear and tear allowance you can also claim a limited renewals allowance. This is based on the net cost of renewing or repairing fixtures that are an integral part of the buildings. The net cost means the cost of the replacement less any amount received for the old item.

Fixtures integral to the building are those that are not normally removed by either tenant or owner if the property is vacated or sold. This will include baths, sinks toilets etc. Any expenditure on renewing these would usually be deductible as an expense (provided there is no element of improvement to the fixture)

Capital allowances

There are lots of different types of capital allowances however property investors would be looking at 'plant and machinery' allowances.

Capital allowances can be claimed on plant or machinery used in a rental business. This includes:

cars,
tools,
office equipment used in running the rental business,
fixtures.

What it doesn't cover though is any of the furniture or other items actually used in a furnished let property. So the beds, sofas, TV etc won't qualify for any tax relief.

Where it is due, you will qualify for a 100% allowance on expenditure up to £25,000 (excluding cars) with the remainder then qualifying for a 18% allowance per year.

Furnished Holiday Lettings

Furnished holiday lettings aren't subject to the capital allowance restriction that applies to normal property lets.

Therefore you'd be looking at claiming Plant and Machinery allowances on all assets used for the purpose of the furnished holiday let property.

This would include:

•vehicles,
•tools used for maintenance,
•office equipment used in running the rental business,
•furniture in the FHL property
•fixtures in the FHL property.

They couldn't claim the wear and tear allowance and would need to decide whether to claim the renewals basis or capital allowances.

6. MAXIMISING CAPITAL ALLOWANCES TO REDUCE RENTAL PROFITS

Everybody knows that you should claim all your allowable expenses in order to minimise your tax bill. This applies to all sorts of income, but particularly to residential lets, where the rental income can be totally eliminated in many cases by maximising deductions for interest, repairs and other deductions.

A type of deduction that is often overlooked is the relief for capital allowances, probably because the legislation does restrict the amount of relief you can obtain. However there are still tax savings to be had, and therefore it's well worth considering.

What are capital allowances?

Capital allowances are a form of tax relief when you purchase capital assets.

When you pay for something in connection with your tenanted property it will either be a revenue item or a capital item. If it's a revenue item it will be deducted when you calculate the profits for the rental business. If it's an allowable tax deduction (eg it was for the purposes of the rental business) it will then be deductible when calculating your tax bill. If it's not deductible (eg its for your own personal use) it will be 'added back' and disallowed for tax purposes.

When you buy capital items the amount you pay will not be deducted when you calculate your profits. This is on the basis that a capital asset will be used in the business for many years, and as such the tax relief should be spread over a number of years.

This is where capital allowances come in. They provide for a fixed rate of relief for different capital expenditure. The amount of relief will depend on the type of asset but relief can vary from 100% to 10%.

In the case of a residential lettings business the main relief will be plant and machinery allowances.

Plant or machinery is not comprehensively defined but in the case of a rental business common examples will include:

•vehicles,
•any tools used for repairing and maintaining the properties,
•office equipment used in running the business such as computers, fax etc
•fixtures in a let property.

Crucially the tax legislation does not allow a capital allowance claim for any furniture and household equipment provided for use by tenants in residential furnished lettings. Therefore any furniture or fixtures that you put into let property will not qualify for capital allowances (as this will usually be accounted for as part of the wear and tear allowance).

You'll therefore need to ensure that you maximise reliefs on all o the assets used for the property business, that aren't actually use in the property itself. The most common asset here will be computer system that is used exclusively for business use (eg t keep a track of rental payments, prepare accounts etc).

For most people the annual investment allowance will exempt u to £250,000 of plant and machinery investments between 1 Janua 2013 – 1 January 2015.

Allowances For Building Owners

The restriction against claiming on furniture and furnishings in let property only applies to a 'dwelling house'. A dwelling house a building, or part of a building, which is a person's home.

Therefore anything that is not a dwelling house could potentially open the door to a claim for capital allowances on the assets actually in the property.

Importantly a block of flats is not a dwelling house, although the actual flats within the block may well be.

This means that a person who owns a block of flats, could claim capital allowances on capital additions to the fabric of the building (provided they are classed as plant or machinery). So the types of things that could be claimed include:

•Cookers, washing machines, dishwashers, refrigerators etc for communal areas
•Lifts
•Sound insulation
•Computer, telecommunication and surveillance systems
•Refrigeration or cooling equipment
•Fire alarm systems; sprinkler and other equipment for extinguishing fires
•Burglar alarm systems
•Partition walls, where moveable and intended to be moved

Energy Savings Allowances

This is a scheme that allows landlords to claim capital allowances when they install:

•Loft insulation,
•Cavity wall insulation,
•Solid wall insulation,
•Draught-proofing
•Insulating hot water systems.
•Floor insulation (from 6 April 2007)

Flat Conversion Allowances

This is not an allowance that the typical property investor will claim, but it will impact on those that look to develop properties and then let them.

In essence, the purpose of this relief is to encourage the conversion of empty space above shops and other commercial premises to residential use. It is a very generous relief as it allows relief for 100% of the capital expenditure incurred in connection with the conversion of the building.

This can be a pretty significant relief and therefore if you're considering converting such premises it will be well worth it to take detailed advice.

As you'd expect there are restrictions which would all need to be looked at in detail, including:

•The flats must be available for short-term letting
•Allowances are not available if the flats that are created are high value.

A flat is classed as high value if the rent that could be generated from the flat exceeds certain specified limits. The current limits are:

Number of rooms in flat elsewhere	Flats in Greater	London Flats
1 or 2 rooms week	£350 per week	£150 pe
3 rooms week	£425 per week	£225 pe
4 rooms week	£480 per week	£300 pe

When looking at the number of rooms you can ignore kitchens an bathrooms, and closets, cloakrooms and hallways not exceeding square meters.

•The property in which the flats are situated must have been bui before 1980.

•The property must not have more than 4 storeys above the ground floor (including an attic if it can be lived in).

•When the property was constructed, the floors above the ground floor should have been used mainly for residential use. The upper floors must have been either unoccupied, or used only for storage, for at least one year before the conversion work starts.

There are also other cases where special rules may apply such as furnished holiday lettings.

If your business qualifies as a furnished holiday letting business one of the big advantages is that you can claim capital allowances on the cost of fitting it out for tenants use (eg chairs, tables, cooker, fridge, television etc).

It's therefore well worth having a think about the type of allowances that you'll be able to claim for your residential property business.

7. SETTING UP YOUR OWN PROPERTY MANAGEMENT COMPANY TO REDUCE TAX

In the past it used to be a pretty popular tax planning opportunity. You'd retain ownership of your rental properties in your own name and set up a property service company.

The company would assist in finding tenants, collecting rents, undertake repairs etc (in other words the activities that would usually be undertaken by an independent property management company). In exchange the company would be paid an agency fee for providing the services (usually 10-15%).

The main advantage of this was that a few years ago a company could earn profits of up to £10,000 free of corporation tax. So the main idea behind the connected service company was to take advantage of the company's tax free band.

The rules have now changed, with companies being taxed o profits up to £300,000 at 20%. The main rate of corporation tax i now 21%.

Given this, it's worth asking, 'is the property service company sti a good idea?'

Well not surprisingly they're not as attractive now as they once were, but given the right circumstances they can still be useful.

Corporation Tax

The corporation tax rate for small companies is now 20%. comparison if you own properties personally and are a higher ra taxpayer you'll be taxed at 40% on the rental profits. So principle a service company can be attractive as you're essential swapping profits taxable at 40% for profits taxable at 20%.

The tax saving is even greater if you have income above £150,000 and pay tax at the additional rate (45%).

This though is only the case provided you don't take profits out of the company, or at least you don't take them out while you're a higher rate/additional rate taxpayer. If you took profits out as dividends (the most common option) you'd suffer an additional 25%/30.55% tax charge on you, personally eliminating the benefit of using the company.

Therefore using the service company could be attractive where:

•You are retaining profits within the company long term - perhaps to start a future trading activity

•You plan to extract profits from the company in the future when you are a basic rate taxpayer. If for example you are a higher rate taxpayer now, but would plan to retire in five years time at which point you would be a basic rate taxpayer, using the service company could be attractive. Any dividends extracted within the basic rate tax band would be free of any additional income tax liability for you. Therefore the net effect of this would be that you'd have only suffered the 20% corporation tax charge, as opposed to an earlier 40% income tax charge.

You are currently UK resident but plan to move overseas in the uture and remain non resident for more than 5 tax years. If this is he case providing you make sure you establish yourself as non UK esident you would be able to extract the cash from the company ree of any further UK income tax charge.

ere's an example illustrating a couple of these points:

xample

rank owns 5 investment properties generating rental profits of 50,000 per tax year. Assuming he is a higher rate taxpayer, he'd y income tax of £20,000 on this.

Over the next five years the income remains the same and then he emigrates to New Zealand. His total income tax bill would be £100,000 over the five years.

If he used a service company, he could use the company to process all payments and deal with the tenants. The company would pay Frank 85% of the profits and retain the other 15%. Frank would therefore receive £42,500, and the company would retain the other £7,500. Frank would pay income tax of £17,000. Assuming the company bears all the expenses it would pay corporation tax of £1,500).

After the five tax years the company would have retained cash of around £30,000 which could then be extracted from the company free of UK income tax as he's a non resident. This may also be free of of New Zealand income tax under their new tax rules for immigrants.

The tax bill, if the company was used, would be around £93,000 There would therefore be a tax saving of around £7K in this case Not massive, but it would more than cover the costs of using the company. In addition if the rents were higher the benefit of using the company would be higher.

Why not just have company ownership?

You could of course just have the company own the propertie outright. Then all of the rental profits would be subject to the lowe rates of corporation tax. Providing one of the cases above applie (ie and there was no tax charge on extraction of the profits) the there could be a significant tax saving.

For example in the case above, rental profits of £50,000 woul result in a corporation tax charge of £10,000 per year. Over th five years this would total £50,000, and if the cash in the compan (£200,000) was extracted free of further tax, there would be a ta saving of around £50,000 when compared to personal ownershi The tax saving when compared to owning and using a servi company would be around £43K.

This is a massive tax saving and well worth considering, the only downside to this is the position when you sell the property.

Capital gains treatment

If you own it personally you'll be entitled to offset the annual CGT exemption on disposal (£11,000, but this could be doubled if you transfer an interest in the property to your spouse), as well as PPR relief if you occupy it and the 18/28% rate of CGT. In addition if you leave the UK and sell up, you could avoid paying any CGT. The fact that you use the company to handle the tenants would not impact on the CGT position and no gain would arise to the company instead it would all be taxed on you.

Contrast this with the position if you opt for full company ownership. The company will get no annual exemption, no PPR relief and no non residency exemption, as well as being subject to the corporation tax rates and not the 18/28% rate of CGT (which could in itself be attractive particularly where the corporation tax is payable at 20% or 21% in the future and your personal CGT rate would be 28%). The only relief in this case would be indexation relief to take account for the effects of inflation but this is unlikely to be significant.

Of course you could always structure this as a share disposal (ie sell the shares in the company rather than the underlying properties) to take account of the 18/28% CGT rate, the annual exemptions and any non UK residency. The downside to this is that any purchaser would be likely to want a discount on the purchase price to reflect the inherent tax liability in the company.

So Which Is Best Then?

Which matters most to you (ie income v capital) is for you to decide. However, looking at the company, many gains will be significant. As such the proceeds may well be large and extracting annually to utilise any remaining basic rate tax band may not be feasible. Therefore the best option in this case would be to become non resident and extract proceeds free of income tax.

Of course if you'd owned personally and had become non resident you'd get a complete CGT exemption, rather than paying corporation tax at 20% on the gain. As such you'd need to weigh up the difference between the CGT saving and the saving in income tax on rental income.

The only difference is that for income tax you wouldn't have to remain non resident for five years.

Looking at the example above, if Frank sold the properties for £750,000 realising a gain of £500,000 after five years if he'd owned personally he could avoid CGT in full if he was non UK resident. Even if he sold whilst he was UK resident (or if for example failed to meet the five year requirement) he'd be taxed at the 28% rate of CGT. Assuming annual CGT exemptions of £11,000 each for him and his wife (if she was a higher rate taxpayer) they would have a CGT charge of £133,840.

If he'd owned the properties via a company the company would pay tax on the profits of:

300,000 @ 20% = 60,000
200,000 @ 21% = 42,000
Total = £102,000

So in this case the company would pay more tax than an individua and the cash would still need to be extracted. If you were stayin as a UK resident, the extra 25% tax charge on any amount received over your basic rate tax band would be likely to make th company less desirable (and if you were to try and take th proceeds out in small amounts per tax year in this case it woul take you around 15 years to take out the full proceeds assumin you had no other income at all).

Therefore using the company would only really be attractive in th case if you were non UK resident. Of course if you were to extra it tax free as a non resident you'd then need to consider the trade off, such as:

If you could own property and obtain the CGT exemption on disposal (as well as avoiding overseas CGT when you sell) you probably wouldn't want to use the company route, as you'd save tax on rental income but you'd pay extra tax on the disposal of £102,000.

Clearly, if the properties qualified for additional reliefs, such as principal private residence relief, this would also swing it in favour of owning personally as opposed to using a company.

What you need to do to use the property service company option?

The most important aspect is that all dealings between you, the company and the tenants are on an arms length basis. This means that the agency fee the company charges you should be set at a similar level to the fee that other independent agents would charge. You should therefore ensure you research the rates that local agents would charge for the same services the company will be providing you, and stick to this. Retain any evidence supporting this in case you need to back up the arms length nature of the agreement.

Keep all books and records for the company separate. If you undertake any services for the company you can certainly bill the company for your time although you will then need to account for income tax and NI on the receipts.

Ensure that the company is structured as a trading operation. If the Revenue was successful in arguing it was an investment activity, this would be disastrous as they'd probably class the company as a close investment company. In this case the tax rate would be 21% as opposed to 20%, and this would not make the company anywhere as attractive. The above actions would help to indicate it was a genuine trade but if you could also obtain any third party agency contracts this would then seal it, and ensure there was no possible risk of an investment company argument.

8. RENTAL LOSSES AND USING A PROPERTY COMPANY TO REDUCE TAX

Companies holding property have particular benefits when profits aren't to be extracted from the company (therefore no income tax charge on extraction) and where you're looking at an investment return in the form of rental income, rather than capital gains. In that case the 40% income tax rate is much higher than the 20%/21% rate of corporation tax and using a company can be worthwhile.

Impact of losses

If you have a rental business making substantial losses using a company can be very attractive.

Rental losses for an individual are just offset against other rental profits either of the same year or of future years. There is no scope o offset the losses against other income (eg employment income, rading income or other investment income).

or a company though, rental losses have a much wider offset. hey can be offset against the total profits of the company. Total rofits includes all other income and capital gains.

his is a huge benefit as it means if you were to sell any of the roperties when the market picks up again, using a company could llow you to offset the losses against the capital gain.

any gains in the company are less than the £300,000 small mpanies rate and losses are substantial this means that using a mpany could easily lead to a lower corporation tax charge than if u'd held personally and been subject to capital gains tax.

Of course you would still need to extract cash from the company. If you can arrange for this to be done free of further taxes (eg by extracting within the basic rate band or as a non UK resident) you can effectively 'lock in' the tax savings.

No better time to set up a property company?

The reduced property prices mean that its never been a better time to transfer property to a property company. If you did want to transfer loss making properties to a company this would be a disposal for CGT purposes. However, the reduced property prices will significantly reduce any capital gains.

Tax-free loan account

Another benefit that shouldn't be forgotten is that by transferring property to the company you can leave the proceeds outstanding and create a tax free loan account. This can be extracted free of income tax and national insurance at any point in the future.

So for any loss making properties, using a company can provide you with many more options to reduce your UK property taxes.

9. HOW A LEASE PREMIUM IS TAXED

In essence, the key issue is deciding whether the receipt should be classed as a form of disposal proceeds, in which case capital gains tax ('CGT')would apply, or whether it should be classed as rental income.

For most people capital treatment will be more beneficial. This is because the annual exemption will be available and the CGT rates are lower than the rates of income tax.

The tax legislation distinguishes between capital and income treatment by looking at the length of the lease term. A premium paid for a very long lease is clearly a capital sum, as this is treated as a part disposal of the underlying freehold interest. In this case there would be a charge to capital gains tax.

If a premium is paid for a shorter lease it has a character more like rent (albeit rent paid in a lump sum rather than periodically). It is more akin to income, and the shorter the lease, the more like income it is.

The tax legislation achieves this balance by charging a proportion of a premium to tax as income. The proportion to be charged as income depends on the length of the lease. The shorter the lease, the greater the proportion to be charged. If the lease is for more than 50 years then none of the premium is treated as income.

The method of calculation of the income element is laid out in the tax legislation, which states that the amount of the premium to be treated as rent (ie income) is based on the following formula:

* 50-Y/50

represents the premium and Y the number of complete years in the term of the lease apart from the first.

Therefore on the basis of a 2 year lease, the premium of £96,000 would be split into income of £94,080 and capital of £1,920. Assuming the landlord was not a property dealer, this would be a capital gain in the landlords hands, although if he had the annual CGT exemption to offset, this would in practice eliminate any CGT charge. The income of £94,080 would simply be treated as additional rental income and be taxed along with other rental income for the landlord.

In terms of reducing the charge, the options are limited, but one option always worth considering is the length of the lease and in particular, whether the length of the lease was longer.

If the terms of the lease include provisions under which the tenant can give notice to extend the lease beyond a certain date, you may take into account any circumstances that make it likely that it will in fact be extended.

Therefore if a lease is renewable for a further period, the Revenue may take into account any circumstances that make it likely that it will be extended when they consider the length of the lease for the purposes of the treatment of premiums.

As such if you could show that the length of the lease is likely tc be for a longer period, this would increase the capital element. Fo example, if the in the example above the lease period wa increased to four years, the taxable income element would b £90,240, and the capital element £5,760. The capital elemen should still be covered by the annual CGT exemption (assuming n other gains in the tax year).

Another aspect is to consider relief for the payment of a premiun If the payer of the premium is using the property for busines purposes, then relief is given in computing the business profit spread over the period of the lease.

However, if the payer sublets the property and does charge premium, the relief first reduces the charge on the premiu received, with any balance of relief due spread over the period of the sublease (similarly if the property is sublet with no premium received, there will be some relief spread over the period of the sublease).

As such if the landlord in this case has sublet the property, and paid a premium to the headlessor to grant the lease, the landlord would receive relief for the income element (eg £94,080 or £90,240) as against the premium paid.

10. ARE YOU A PROPERTY TRADER OR INVESTOR?

Property investment in both UK, and overseas has become very popular. We're seeing increasing numbers of people looking at carrying this out as a full time activity, but right at the start it's important to get some sound advice so you start off on the right footing. In particular, the distinction is often blurred between someone simply investing in a buy to let property, and someone buying a property with the intention to 'do it up'.

It goes without saying that you don't want your profit to be eaten up by tax, so you will be looking to identify whether there are ways to reduce the amount of tax you'll have to pay.

Tax Treatment

The first point to consider would be how this activity will be treated for tax purposes. There are broadly two options, either trea it as a capital transaction or as a trading transaction.

If the intention in purchasing the property was to develop and sel the property with the intention of making a profit, the Revenu would be likely to argue that you are a property trader. By contras capital transactions are usually retained for property investment eg an individual purchasing a property to rent out.

The distinction impacts on how any 'profit' is treated and taxed. property trader would be subject to income tax on any profi whereas the disposal of a property investment would be subject capital gains tax ('CGT') on any gain arising.

In some circumstances trader treatment can be benefici particularly as it allows for a greater offset of expenses. Wheth the Revenue would agree that this is a capital transaction w depend on a number of issues, including:

•Whether you have undertaken this kind of activity before
•How long the property will be held prior to disposal
•Will the properties will be rented out
•Whether you anticipate doing this again

If the Revenue will accept that this is a capital transaction, this would allow you to utilise the various CGT reliefs such as the annual exemption and principal private residence ('PPR' relief) and therefore for most people this will be the most attractive treatment.

A key issue would be how you treated the property after development. If you were to dispose of it within 12-24 months, there would be a good argument that income tax treatment would apply. There would then be fewer reliefs, and no benefit would be obtained from living in the property as you couldn't claim PPR relief in any case. In order to rebut any such argument, you would need to persuade the Revenue that the property was purchased with the intention of living in it, or obtaining tenants, but circumstances subsequently changed (eg personal/financial issues) changed and the property needed to be sold.

By contrast, if you were to lease the property for a number of years after development, or if this was an isolated activity you would have a good argument that the property was not purchased/developed solely to resell at a profit, and CGT should be applied.

If you were classed as a property trader, you would also need to consider any national insurance charge which is set at 9% on profits within the upper NIC limit (broadly equivalent to the basic rate income tax band) and 2% above this. There could also be a liability to NIC on the profits if you were classed as a trader.

For most people that are just starting off, it would be advisable where possible to argue for capital treatment. The gain would be calculated as the disposal proceeds less the costs of acquisition/development and enhancement (eg refurbishment expenditure). You would also be allowed a deduction for the incidental costs of acquisition and disposal (eg stamp duty, estate agents fees, conveyancing fees).

You would then obtain the benefit of the annual exemption on disposal.

You could also consider occupying the property and claiming PPR relief. This is very advantageous and 12 months occupation could eliminate three years worth of the gain. If the property was clearly purchased, developed and then immediately sold none of these reliefs would be available.

11. REDUCING CGT WITH PPR RELIEF

Anyone owning a buy to let property will be looking to reduce capital gains tax on a future disposal.

One of the most popular ways to do this is to occupy it as a main residence before disposal.

What benefits do you get?

If you do establish a property as a main residence you can then claim principal private residence ('PPR') relief. This will reduce any gain based on:

Period of occupation as a main residence/Period of ownership

When counting the period of occupation the last 36 months is always included. Therefore you can qualify for partial PPR relief dependent on the period of ownership.

For instance, if you owned a property for 5 years and then occupied for 1 year before selling it, you'd get PPR relief of 3/6 (50%).

In addition you'd also get lettings relief to further reduce the gain. This provides for a further CGT exemption for the lower of:

Amount of PPR relief
Gain attributable to the letting
£40,000

Therefore occupying a buy to let property as a main residence before selling can be very effective in reducing the amount of CGT.

Principal Private residence ('PPR') relief exempts a proportion of the gain on a property, when the property disposed of has been the owners main residence.

Therefore to qualify for this relief two conditions need to be satisfied:

- the property must be occupied as a residence, and
- it must be the main residence

In order to be a residence you need to own an interest in the property. This can be either a freehold or leasehold interest - but not a licence.

Of key importance to many is how long it is necessary to occupy a property for before it can qualify as a residence/main residence. Residence is not defined in the legislation, however the Revenue expect a degree of permanence, therefore occupation for only a handful of days each year would not constitute residence.

Whilst drawn from a different context a Revenue extra statutory concession used to suggest that a period of occupation of not less than three months is required to establish a property as the only or main residence.

There are no hard and fast rules as to how long to occupy the property before it can be classed as a residence. Some commentators suggest occupying a property for a period of 12 months, although there is no fixed period set by the Revenue and they frequently refer to the 'quality' as opposed to the 'quantity' of the occupation. It is important to ensure that the residence is genuine. For example the property should be your registered address for the electoral register, and your employers should be informed of the new address

It's a matter of fact when a property is a residence, a tax inspector will look at the whole circumstances surrounding the occupation of the property. The checklist below highlights some of the key factual issues to consider.

Issues to take into account when considering whether a property is a main residence includes:

- Is the Property a freehold property?
- Are the utility bills etc addressed to you?
- Was there continuous and regular occupation of the property by you?
- Was the house the family home?
- Did your tax return/Revenue correspondence go to this property?
- Did letters from your employer go to this property?
- Did you work close to this property?
- Are any bills for work etc billed to this property?
- Is the property registered as your main residence with the local authority?
- Was this property furnished with your furniture

Of course for most people this won't even be an issue. They will own one property and this will be the main residence. What if they own two or more properties though? Well this is when you'd need o look at the matters as highlighted above to try and see which of he properties was the main residence.

f you've got a property that is let and you're looking to reduce the apital gains tax charge on the future disposal a popular option is o consider occupying it as a main residence. In this case it would hen qualify for at least partial principal private residence ('PPR') elief as well as lettings relief.

f this applies to you, you'd again need to consider the above and ctually make sure it was your home for a suitable period (say 6-12 onths +) prior to a disposal to ensure the property was a main esidence.

hanges To PPR Relief

s we've seen above, providing you've occupied a property as a ain residence, you can qualify for the last 3 years of deemed occupation when calculating any Principal Private Residence relief. This applies even if you don't actually occupy the property and have a new main residence.

However, in the 2013 Autumn Statement the Chancellor stated that they propose to reduce the 3 year deemed occupation to 18 months as from April 2014. We shall have to wait for further details to assess precisely how this will impact on disposals after 5 April 2014, however in the final chapter we look at some of the issues arising.

12. IS LETTING A PROPERTY BENEFICIAL TO REDUCE CGT?

There are two main tax reasons why letting a property may be advantageous. These are:

•Firstly to assist in demonstrating an investment motive.

Where you buy a property with the intention of selling it, any gain on the disposal will be assessed as taxable profit. This means that it won't be subject to capital gains tax, but will instead be subject to income tax.

This is generally not to your benefit. Unless you had significant trading losses or had a lot of expenditure that you could offset when calculating the profits (you can offset more expenses for income tax than capital gains tax), being subject to CGT will reduce the tax charge. Not only will you have the annual CGT exemption, there is also no potential national insurance charge and he tax rate is fixed 18% - 28%. By contrast income tax could be charged at rates of 20 - 45%.

You'll be subject to income tax if you're a property trader, and apital gains tax if you're a property investor. Property investors enerally buy property to let or hold for another investment motive eg capital appreciation) whereas property traders will look to buy roperty with the intention of selling at a profit (usually quickly nd possibly after developing or renovating it).

herefore letting a property can be advantageous in demonstrating n investment as opposed to trading motive. This would though eed to be a genuine activity. You couldn't for example buy a operty in January, agree to sell it in June and then arrange a tting in between to show an investment motive.

Where a property was previously a main residence

Where a property was previously a main residence you can claim principal private residence relief to reduce the capital gains tax on disposal.

However in addition to PPR relief, if a main residence was let, you can claim lettings relief. This will further reduce any capital gain on the disposal.

It doesn't matter when the letting was. Whether it's before or after the period of occupation by you, you'll still qualify for lettings relief. Lettings relief is given as the lower of:

•The amount of PPR relief
•£40,000
•The gain attributable to the letting

Therefore in the straightforward case where you occupied a property as a main residence and then let it for the period that yo weren't occupying it, the gain attributable to the letting would b the gain after PPR relief.

If you had a property vacant for a while before occupying it an also letting it, at some point you would need to allocate the gain t the letting and period of occupation for calculating lettings relie and PPR relief. This allocation would usually be done on a pro rat basis. Therefore to calculate the gain attributable to the letting yo would calculate:

Period of letting/Period of ownership * Gain before PPR relief

Lettings relief provides for an exemption of up to £40,000 but th is per person. Therefore if you and your spouse jointly own property on which you can both claim PPR relief, you'll bo qualify for lettings relief at up to £40,000 each. This tax relief of further £80,000 is a significant deduction and is a valuable bene of letting a main residence.

If the property has not been occupied as a main residence thoug letting it will not qualify for any capital gains tax deductions. As such if you have a property that has been let throughout it's period of ownership it may be worthwhile considering occupying it as a main residence before disposal.

Occupying as a main residence

If you occupied a property for 6-12 months you should be able to establish it as your main residence. The effect on lettings relief would depend on the period of ownership and size of the gain arising.

By occupying for 12 months you'd obtain the last 36 months deemed occupation. Therefore if you'd owned the property for 10 years, you'd get PPR relief of 30%. If the property was let throughout the other 9 years the gain attributable to the letting would clearly exceed the gain due for PPR relief, therefore your lettings relief would be the lower of PPR relief and £40,000.

Whether you'll get the full £40,000 or a lesser amount of lettings relief would primarily then depend on the size of the gain.

If the gain was £100,000 for example, PPR relief would be £30,000 and this would also be the amount of Lettings relief.

If the gain was £150,000, PPR relief would be £45,000, and lettings relief would be £40,000.

Occupying a let property as a main residence can therefore be effective in reducing CGT, but the amount of the reduction will depend on the period of ownership (shorter period - more relief) and the size of the gain (higher gain - more relief).

13. MAXIMISING PRIVATE LETTINGS RELIEF TO REDUCE CGT

Lettings relief is not as well known as principal private residence relief, however where it applies it can be very effective in further reducing your capital gains tax charge.

Lettings relief applies only where:

•You can claim principal private residence relief, and

•You have at some point let out the property

Claiming PPR relief

In order to claim PPR relief you need to have occupied the property as your main residence. This could be by actually occupying it as your main residence or by occupying two properties as residences and electing one as the main residence.

Where you've occupied a property as a main residence the amount of PPR relief is calculated as:

Period of occupation as a main residence/Period of ownership

In all cases the last 36 months is classed as deemed occupation.

How lettings relief works

Lettings relief gives another capital gains tax exemption for a amount equivalent to the lower of:

•The amount of PPR relief

•£40,000

•The gain attributable to the letting

What does this mean?

Effectively:

•The highest amount of lettings relief you'll get is £40,000

•If the amount of PPR relief is less than £40,000 you'll get another deduction for the amount of PPR relief

•If you've occupied a property for a period and simply let it for the remaining period the gain after PPR relief will be the gain attributable to the letting.

In this case providing the property has been occupied for most of the period of ownership, the remaining gain will be covered by lettings relief providing it's less than £40,000.

If the property has not been either occupied as a main residence or let for the entire period of ownership (eg it's been left empty or used for a business purpose) you'd need to calculate the gain attributable to the letting to assess the amount of PPR relief. This is usually calculated as:

Period of letting/Period of ownership * Gain before PPR relief

'o maximise the amount of lettings relief you should look arefully at:

Timings of the disposal - particularly with reference to the mount of PPR relief. If the gain attributable to the letting is more ıan £40,000 you need to be careful as to the amount of PPR relief ıd that this does not unduly restrict the amount of lettings relief.

this case by maximising the amount of PPR relief you are also aximising the amount of lettings relief as the two reliefs will be e same.

In many cases it will be more beneficial to arrange for a quick disposal rather than retaining the property and renting it out for another couple of years.

If for example a property was occupied for 2 years and then let for the remaining 8 years it would make sense to sell ASAP to maximise the reliefs.

An immediate disposal would give PPR relief of:

Period of occupation = 2 years + last 3 years deemed occupation = 5 years

Period of ownership = 10 years

PPR relief = 50%

If the gain was £80,000 PPR relief would be £40,000. Lettings relief would eliminate the gain of £40,000.

If a disposal was left for 5 years PPR relief would be:

Period of occupation = 2 years + last 36 months deeme occupation = 5 years

Period of ownership = 15 years

PPR relief = 33.3%

If the gain was £80,000 PPR relief would be £26,400, leaving gain of £53,600. Lettings relief would cover £40,000 leavin £13,600 charged to CGT (before other exemptions may b applied).

•Transfer to a spouse

Lettings relief is given on a per person basis. Therefore it can oft be beneficial to own assets jointly to maximise the amount lettings relief.

This would be the case if the amount of PPR relief and gain attributable to the letting is more than £40,000.

Note though that you would need to split the gain between the relevant owners. When looking at each owners capital gain they would each calculate PPR relief and consider whether the remaining gain would qualify for lettings relief.

Making use of this £40,000 exemption can be very attractive in reducing CGT.

A popular mechanism here is to transfer a property into joint names allowing both the husband and wife to utilise the £40,000 limit. This then doubles the amount of lettings relief to £80,000.

14. IS IT WORTH REOCCUPYING A PROPERTY BEFORE SALE TO REDUCE CGT?

If you have a property that has been occupied as a main residence by you at any time in your period of ownership you'll be able to claim principal private residence ('PPR') relief on the disposal.

This will then reduce the amount of CGT that you pay. PPR relief is given based on the following:

Period of occupation/Period of ownership

So if you occupy it for 5 years and you've owned it for 10 you'll get 50% PPR relief.

However when taking into account the period of occupation yo are always deemed to have occupied it for the last 3 years o ownership (providing it was your main residence at some othe point in your ownership).

Therefore if you purchased it in 2003 and sold it in 2013 you'v have owned it for 10 years. If you occupied it between 2006 - 200 you'd have 3 years of actual occupation and also have the 3 year deemed occupation (total 6 years and therefore 60% PPR relief i this case).

If you occupied it between 2011 - 2013 you'd have 3 yea occupation. Why? Well because the last 3 years deemed ownershi (2010 - 2013) would cover the period of actual occupation in ar case.

So based on this in many cases there would be no benefit to gained by reoccupying a property before disposal - as you' already deemed to be occupying it.

Of course if you've never previously occupied the property as main residence it may be advantageous to occupy it as a main residence before disposal (eg for 6-12 months) as this would then entitle you to the last 36 months of deemed occupation. This would therefore increase your amount of PPR relief (and therefore lower your CGT) significantly.

Other deemed periods

There is, however, another case where it can be very beneficial to reoccupy a property prior to the disposal.

Where you work overseas (or in certain other special cases eg if you work away in the UK) you can be deemed to have occupied the property for your period of absence (even if it's rented) providing:

• You have no other residence overseas, and
• You occupy the property both before and after the period of absence.

So if you have no other residence (which means no other freehold or leasehold property eg employer provided accommodation) you may want to look to reoccupy a property before the disposal. This could then ensure that the period of your absence was completely exempt from CGT.

The periods that qualify for this special treatment are:

Any period when working abroad
Up to 4 years if working away in the UK
Up to 3 years for any other purpose

15. CLAIMING PPR RELIEF IF YOU CONVERT A HOUSE INTO FLATS

The key relief when you are looking at converting a residential house into flats may be Principal Private Residence relief.

The tax legislation states that Principal Private Residence relief is available where a gain arises from the disposal of an interest in a dwelling house or part of a dwelling house which has at some time been its owners only or main residence.

In most cases the whole of a building in which an individual lives will be a dwelling house. But in some cases the dwelling house may be more than one building or only part of a building.

If you have converted a house into flats it would therefore need to be considered what constituted the 'dwelling house' - either the entire property or just the individuals flats.

The most common example of a dwelling house which is only part of a building in which it is situated, is a flat in a block of flats Each flat is a self-contained unit and is itself regarded as a dwelling house and not part of a dwelling house.

The Revenue have stated that '…There are also buildings which to outward appearances are a single dwelling house but which are in fact split up into self-contained units. Each self-contained unit is itself a dwelling house…'

If therefore each flat had separate facilities such as bathroom kitchen, bedrooms, etc there would be little prospect of arguing that they were not separate dwelling houses.

On this basis in order to obtain PPR relief on the disposal of th flats you would have needed to have actually occupied them as main residence. If, for example, you were to occupy a flat for period as a main residence before moving into one of the other flats, you could then claim PPR relief on the disposal.

Therefore, if you converted a house into 3 flats and you occupied flat 1 and then flat 2 these would qualify for PPR relief on a disposal. This is based on the ratio of:

Period of occupation/Period of ownership

In both cases the last 36 months of ownership would be deemed to be occupied by you.

In addition in respect of the two flats that you actually occupied as a main residence you could claim lettings relief if they were let at any point in your period of ownership.

This would provide for a further exemption for the lower of:

- £40,000
- PPR relief
- The gain attributable to the letting

n essence therefore, if each flat is regarded as a separate dwelling ouse you would need to apportion the gain between the flats sold nd then calculate PPR relief and lettings relief for the disposal of lats actually occupied (eg 1 & 2).

he gains would then all be consolidated and the annual exemption vould then be offset to provide your chargeable gain.

ny flats that you didn't occupy could be faced with a CGT charge n the disposal. It's also worth noting that there is anti avoidance gislation that can prevent PPR relief applying where there is xpenditure incurred for the purposes of realizing a gain. As such nting or occupying the property would assist in demonstrating at this was not the case.

you can obtain full PPR relief on the disposal, it would not need be disclosed to the Revenue.

16. QUALIFYING FOR ROLLOVER RELIEF ON COMPLULSORY PURCHASES

It's well known that there's a rollover relief that provides for any capital gains on certain business assets to be deferred when you spend the proceeds on other business assets.

For property investors this will not apply, as in order to qualify, the properties need to be used for the purposes of a trade. As most property investors won't be carrying out a trade from their investment properties, they won't get rollover relief when they sell.

However, there is another capital gains tax deferral technique that can apply to property investors. Where investment properties are compulsory purchased (eg by a local council) there is a special form of rollover relief that could apply.

Under S247 TCGA there is a rollover relief where land or propert is compulsory purchased. The legislation states that the relief ma be claimed where there is:

a. a disposal of land (referred to as the `old' land),
b. to an authority exercising or having compulsory powers,
c. by any person (referred to as the `landowner') including a individual, trustee or company.

"Authority" is defined in Section 243(5) TCGA 1992 to mean person or body of persons with compulsory purchase powers.

One of the conditions imposed by the Revenue is that th landowner must not have taken any step to make known h willingness to dispose of the old land to the authority or others b advertising or otherwise.

However they will disregard any action taken to make it known, b advertising or otherwise, that you were prepared to sell the land, it occurred more than 3 years before the compulsory acquisition in question.

So you need to ensure that you don't:

•put the house up for sale before being approached by the council
•approach the council yourself

Main residence exemption

The proceeds can be used to purchase any type of land or property. However you need to be careful if you're purchasing more private residences.

New land is excluded from relief if BOTH the following conditions apply:

•the new land comprises a dwelling house, and
•if a disposal of the new land were to occur at any time within a period of six years from the date of its acquisition, the whole or part of the gain on its disposal would not be chargeable because of principal private residence relief.

This means that if you reinvest in property which is, or which becomes within six years, your main residence you can't benefit from the special roll- over relief.

It should also be noted that where you claim the relief, and reinvest in private residential property the Revenue will keep an eye on the land. They have specifically stated:

'..Where new land is acquired which seems suitable for use as a private residence by the new owner but which at the time of the roll-over relief claim is not used as a private residence by the owner, a forward note should be made to review the position at, say, the three or six year points after the date of acquisition in order to ensure that the property has not become the only or main residence of the landowner…'

Time limit

The period during which the new land is to be acquired is the same as for rollover relief. This means that the new land must be:

•acquired, or
•an unconditional contract for the acquisition must be entered into in the period
 - beginning 12 months before or
 - ending three years after

the date of disposal of the old land.

When is the land treated as being sold if there is a compulsory purchase?

The key issue here is the date of disposal. You generally need to ensure that the date of disposal is within the 3 year period as described above.

The date of disposal is usually the date on which the amount of compensation is agreed or determined by a Tribunal.

Where the compulsory purchase is carried out by means of general vesting declaration, the date of disposal is the date on which the declaration becomes effective.

How does the rollover relief apply?

Where the whole of the proceeds received as a result of the compulsory purchase are used to purchase qualifying new land, no immediate gain arises and instead the allowable expenditure on the new land is reduced. The net effect of this is that the gain charged when the new land is sold in the future.

Note that where only part of the proceeds are reinvested there could be a full or partial deferral, depending on the amount of the proceeds retained and the size of the capital gain.

The rollover relief for compulsory purchases can operate as a useful deferral though. It's important to remember that:

- You mustn't approach the council or compulsory purchase provider before they approach you
- You shouldn't advertise the property for sale (except for the 3 year rule as mentioned above)
- You shouldn't occupy as a main residence within 6 years
- ou should carefully calculate the capital gain and ensure that the proceeds reinvested are sufficient to ensure a full rollover relief

17. TAX PLANNING WHEN INVESTING IN UK PROPERTY

We're often asked for tax structuring, where a UK non-resident and non-domiciled individual wish to purchase a UK property. In this chapter we look at some of the tax planning issues and opportunities available.

Jack is resident and domiciled in Spain. He has relatives in the UK and is interested in purchasing a property here because (a) he wants somewhere to stay when he visits and (b) he has heard that UK property prices are set to rise.

The question is, how from a tax perspective should he structure the purchase?

There are broadly two ways to buy the property:

•By using direct ownership, or
•Using some form of intermediary like a trust or company.

Note, we'll assume in this chapter that the property is valued at les than £2,000,000 as otherwise the new Annual Tax On Envelope Dwellings ("ATED") could apply to corporate ownership. I however such a property was used for a genuine Buy To Le business there is specific relief available from these provisions i any case.

We will also ignore the effects of the proposed changes to the CG rules from April 2015. These changes may well have a significa impact on the CGT position after April 2015, however we ar currently waiting for detailed information on the changes fro HMRC.

DIRECT OWNERSHIP

Capital Gains Tax

From a capital gains tax perspective direct ownership is potentially attractive:

•The Principal Private Residence (PPR) relief operates to exempt a gain on the disposal of an individual's main residence. Even if the property is not, on the facts, Jack's main residence, he could certainly submit an election to have it treated as his main residence.

•As he is non-resident, he would not, in any case, be liable to UK capital gains tax on the disposal of any assets.

Inheritance Tax

The inheritance tax position is, however, not as good. The holding of property in the UK would mean that Jack has a UK estate and, as well as probate being required on his death, the house would be subject to inheritance tax to the extent that the value exceeds the £325,000 nil rate band. As the value of the property is expected to rise rapidly, this could result in a significant tax bill, were he to die while still owning the asset.

There are, however, a number of methods available to Jack to reduce or eliminate any inheritance tax charge:

Use of Multiple Ownership

The property could be acquired in multiple ownership. For example, Jack, his wife and children could all own the property jointly.

Provided the individuals have no other UK assets, it is likely that each share will be below the nil rate band.

In order to avoid problems with the 'gift with reservation of benefit' legislation, it is necessary to gift cash to the family members, which they can then use to purchase their shares of the property.

The gift with reservation of benefit (GROB) provisions apply to property in particular, where an interest in a property is given away, yet the person gifting the interest still continues to reside in the property. For inheritance tax purposes, the whole value of the property is still regarded as included in the occupier's estate for inheritance tax purposes.

Gifting of Property

Another solution would be to gift cash to a younger member of the family who can then make the acquisition. The gift will be exempt from inheritance tax, provided the person making the gift survives seven years. The above GROB rules would not apply as the gift was a cash gift. The UK pre-owned assets tax charge should also not be relevant if Jack is non-UK resident.

The property will then belong to the donee (the younger family member) and if the donee were to die, it would be included in his estate for inheritance tax purposes.

Mortgages

The value of an individual's estate is essentially the market valu of the assets at the date of death, less any liabilities outstanding a the date of death.

It is therefore possible to effectively reduce any inheritance ta charge to zero by obtaining a substantial loan against the value c the property. Provided the mortgage reduces the 'net value' of th property to below the nil rate band (currently £325,000), there wi be no inheritance tax payable.

The mortgage funds obtained can be invested overseas and ar interest return would then be exempt from UK income ta provided the interest income is not remitted to the UK.

USING A TRUST TO OWN THE PROPERTY

Capital Gains Tax

The Principal Private Residence relief is extended to situations where a beneficiary is entitled to occupy a house under the terms of a trust deed. In these circumstances, the trustees would be able to claim PPR relief when they sell the property.

In the case of a non-UK domiciliary, as the trustees are non-resident they would not, in any case, be liable to UK capital gains tax.

It would only be if the settlor of the trust (or his close family) was also a beneficiary and became UK resident that the gains of the trust could be attributed to him under the anti-avoidance provisions.

Inheritance Tax

The trust will be subject to special inheritance tax rules. One of the key implications is that it could be subject to an inheritance tax charge every 10 years starting with the date of commencement.

USING AN OFFSHORE COMPANY

The property could be owned by a non-resident company. In this case the non-domiciliary would own the shares in the company.

As the shares are non-UK property, they would be exempt from inheritance tax. Key risks with this are:

The company's residence position may be closely scrutinised by the taxman and it may be difficult to show that the central management and control is exercised outside the UK, particularly if all directors are UK resident and the asset of the company is a UK property. If HMRC is able to successfully argue that the company is UK resident, any gain on the disposal of the property, would be subject to UK corporation tax and no PPR relief would be available.

•In addition, on disposal of the shares in the company, no capital gains tax would be payable by Jack provided he remained non-resident. If he was UK resident, he may not be charged to UK CGT provided the proceeds were retained outside the UK and he was subject to the remittance basis, as he's a non-UK domiciliary.

18. SHOULD YOU USE A COMPANY TO HOLD INVESTMENT PROPERTY?

It's a pretty common question, and is something that should be considered well before you actually buy any property (or even exchange contracts). Note that what we're mainly considering here is the case where someone is buying property to either renovate and sell on or to hold as a buy to let.

If you're just buying property that you will occupy as your main residence, you should almost always buy it in your own name. Why? Well if you're occupying it as your main residence you'll be able to obtain principal private residence ('PPR') relief on a future disposal, which will ensure that any profit you make on the disposal is free of tax.

Aside from this one of the key issues will be whether you would intend to sell developed properties or retain them long term to generate capital growth and rental returns.

In either case the initial consideration will be whether to hold the property via a company or personally. You should generally avoid 'mixing' these. For example, one possible option would be to buy property personally, develop it and then transfer it to a wholly owned limited company which would rent the property out.

This should generally be avoided. If you hold the property in your name, develop it and then transfer to a company, the transfer would be a chargeable disposal for income tax/capital gains tax purposes. The market value of the properties would be likely to be used and any profit/gain would be likely to be taxed on you personally. This could be the case even though the property would then be held by the company long term.

Therefore ideally you would look to establish the correct structure for holding the property from the outset, and either hold personally or transfer the property pre development to the company.

If you were looking to develop properties, any profits would be assessed to income tax. On this basis, and assuming you would be retaining most of the profits within the business, with minimal extractions (ie retaining cash in the business for future use) it would be likely to be more tax efficient to use a company to conduct the trade.

If you carried out the trade personally, you would be taxed at 20/40%/45% on the profits generated when you sold each property. If the profits were significant this would be predominantly at the 40%/45% rate of income tax. This would apply irrespective of whether the proceeds were reinvested into further development properties or not. In addition you could be subject to NIC, at a rate of 9% up to the higher rate tax band, and 2% on additional profits.

By contrast, if you were to use a company, the company could earn profits of up to £300,000 pa and pay corporation tax at 20%.

It's worthwhile noting that if you own any other companies this £300,000 limit is reduced according to the number of companies. For example if you owned one other company the 20% tax band would be reduced to £150,000.

In this case if annual profits would be above this, it may be worthwhile to consider simply carrying out both trades from one company, particularly if the profits of one of the companies is very low. This would then increase the 20% tax band to £300,000.

The company would not be charged to NIC on the profits, but as the company is a separate legal entity you would need to extract cash from the company. If you had provided funds to the company as a loan on the start up, you could extract amounts up to this, free of income tax and NIC. You could also consider taking cash as dividend to utilise any basic rate tax band, again effectively free of income tax.

If you were looking to retain properties long term and benefit from capital growth and rental income, keeping them in your name would be likely to be preferable. In this case you would be classed as a property investor rather than a property trader and the reliefs under CGT for personal as opposed to company ownership would be greater. In addition the tax rate for private investors is now set at 18% or 28%.

If the potential gain would be within your basic rate band personal ownership will lead to a tax saving of at least 2% in the company without even considering the fact that company owners need to get the profits out of the company.

If, as is often the case, the capital gain would be charged at 28%, this is actually more than the rate that would often be paid by a company – assuming that profits were not extracted from the company.

Individual owners do however have the annual CGT exemptions to offset which are currently £11,000 each. So if you owned with your spouse, that's an extra tax deduction of £22,000. A company s only entitled to relief for inflation.

So, if you used a company to hold investment properties the gains on a future disposal would therefore be higher, but the tax rate on he actual gain may be lower. However you would then have the roblem of extracting the large disposal proceeds (unless the roceeds were retained in the company).

n many cases a full extraction of the proceeds would eliminate the enefit of using a company.

lowever, where some or all of the proceeds are to be retained in e company (eg for future reinvestment), using a company to take dvantage of the lower rate of corporation tax may be beneficial.

his assumes that the key consideration would be capital growth. s an investor you would also obtain rental income, which would likely to be taxed at 20/40/45%. In any case if the properties are ghly geared, any rental profits would be unlikely to be significant after the mortgage interest was deducted.

Therefore when considering whether to purchase via a company or personally as a first step you should ensure that you carefully consider the nature of your property activities and whether they will be classed as trading or investment.

19. AVOIDING CGT AND INHERITANCE TAX ON INVESTMENT PROPERTIES

One of the key concerns of anyone with a significant property investment portfolio, is how to avoid the large inheritance tax charge when you ultimately 'meet your maker'.

Of course you could simply give it away, but the problem with investment property is that it may well be showing a large gain since you purchased it. If you transferred it to your children or grandchildren, although you'd avoid IHT after 7 years you could be faced with a large capital gains tax ('CGT') charge on the transfer.

One way to 'have your cake and eat it' could be to use a trust to hold the property. Whether it's established as a discretionary trust or an interest in possession trust doesn't really matter now. Most lifetime trusts will still be 'relevant property trusts' and as such will be subject to the tax regime usually reserved for discretionary trusts. This means that:

- You can transfer properties into the trust free of CGT. Note that it's important the trust isn't for the benefit of you, your wife or minor children, and also that it isn't to be used as a main residence of a beneficiary under the trust.

- The trust can transfer property to beneficiaries in the future free of CGT (as they could make another holdover relief election)

- You can transfer in amount up to your remaining nil rate band free of IHT.

As the nil rate band is £325,000 and assuming you've made no previous transfers when you also take account of the annual exemption(s) this means you could transfer in property with a value of £331,000. For a couple this therefore allows inheritance tax free transfers of property up to £662,000.

You would still need to survive for 7 years for the value transferred to be excluded from your estate. However, providing you satisfy this, the property would be outside your estate and subject to the new tax regime in the trust.

Another caveat here is that you should ensure that you do not retain any benefit in the property transferred. If you received rental income or occupied it occasionally, the gift could be ineffective for tax purposes and the property would remain within your estate.

The trust could therefore be used to arrange for a tax free transfer of investment properties to your adult children.

The trust does not completely avoid inheritance tax. Instead it would be subject to the special regime that applies to discretionary trusts. In particular there would be a tax charge after 10 years in the trust. This would however, be much less than the rate of inheritance tax if owned personally and would be based on the growth in the value of the trust assets over the nil rate bands.

The rate of tax in the trust would be in the region of 3-6%. Ther could therefore be a huge tax saving from using a trust to pass o investment property.

The beauty of this arrangement is that your nil rate bands renew every 7 years, so you could make a transfer of £662,000 in 201 (with your spouse). No IHT would be paid and you could make further substantial settlement of investment property to the trust i 2020.

By using a trust in this way it could allow you to transf investment properties to family members, whilst avoiding an immediate capital gains tax charge. The eventual beneficia would hold the property with your base cost.

Therefore they would crystallise the tax charge when they sell b it's a useful method of avoiding any immediate CGT on a transfer to avoid IHT.

20. BUYING PROPERTY TAX EFFICIENTLY WHILE YOUR CHILDREN ARE STUDYING

The slump in property prices will have made many people consider whether buying property for their children to occupy whilst at university is cost effective.

However, given the currently low prices, if you're looking at the long term with perhaps other family members occupying the property and also renting it out to third parties it can still be a worthwhile investment.

If you were looking to structure such an investment you have three main options:

•Firstly you could purchase in your name

•Secondly you could purchase in your child's name

•Thirdly you could use a trust

Purchasing in your name

If you purchase in your name you obviously have total control over the property, however it is generally a tax inefficient option.

As you haven't occupied the property as a main residence you won't get principal private residence ('PPR') relief on a disposal.

In addition the property will remain within your estate for inheritance tax purposes.

Purchasing in your children's name

There is an immediate inheritance tax advantage as after 7 years the value gifted will be excluded from your estate (provided you don't continue to benefit from the property).

However, the PPR relief position would not be straightforward. If you purchased in the name of one of your children they would only obtain PPR relief to reduce the gain on a disposal for the period that they actually occupied the property. If they occupied the property for say 4 years and then another sibling occupied it there would not be total relief from tax on the disposal.

Even if you purchased the property in multiple names unless they all occupied the property for the entire period of ownership (except for the final 36 months) there would not be full PPR relief. The other disadvantage of purchasing in your children's name is that they would have full control over the property (although you could mitigate this with a charge over the property).

Using a trust

In most cases using a trust would be a very attractive option. It provides for flexibility in terms of the occupation, gives you some element of control and also has significant tax advantages.

Consider the following arrangement:

•You establish a trust and transfer funds into it to buy a property;

•Trustees are appointed to manage the trust - these can be family members if you choose, but you can also appoint a Trustee Company, which is set up specifically to act as a professional trustee

•The trust purchases a property for £300,000 which is then occupied by "child-one" as his / her principal private residence fo three years;

•On graduating "child-one" moves out and the property is let fo two years until "child-two" moves in;

•"Child-two" then occupies for four further years;

The property is then let for six years and finally sold for a gain of £200,000 after ownership for 15 years.

The main benefit is terms of Capital Gains Tax. Assuming CGT is paid at 28%, the tax due would vary considerably. If the property had been bought by:

a. you, the tax would be £44,800;

b. your child, it would be £22,400;

c. the trust, it would be £NIL. As the property is occupied by more than one beneficiary this enables the trust to benefit from a number of aspects of the principal private residence relief whilst also benefiting from letting relief.

The occupation by two children as beneficiaries of the trust enables the trust to relieve a much greater percentage of the chargeable gain and, in this instance, all that remains is then mitigated by letting relief.

f the trust excludes you, then the amount settled by you will drop out of your estate for Inheritance Tax (IHT) purposes after seven years. However, if IHT planning is not an objective of this arrangement, then all the family, including yourself, can be beneficiaries of the trust without losing the CGT advantages and veryone can benefit under the terms of the trust when it comes to ividing up the proceeds.

nother issue is what happens to the property if not sold. Your rst child may have married, and even entered into a divorce. If the apital is advanced when the proceeds are realised, then on ivorce, half of the capital would be lost. If instead, the trustees an the capital to "child one", then on the dissolution of the arriage the capital can be recovered (as it is a debt to the trust) nd, at a later date, the capital can be advanced directly to "child ne".

21. REDUCING CGT, INHERITANCE TAX AND INCOME TAX BY USING MORTGAGES

Although the property prices have reduced significantly in the last few months, many buy to let ('BTL') landlords will still be faced with a large potential inheritance tax charge.

With IHT at 40% on amounts in excess of the nil rate band (£325,000 for 2013/2014) it's easy to see how a substantial IHT liability could arise.

Gifting an interest in the property

The easiest way to avoid IHT is to simply transfer an interest ir property to your children or other family members.

This would be a Potentially Exempt Transfer ('PET') and providec you survived at least 7 years from the date of transfer the valu transferred would be excluded from your estate for inheritance ta purposes. You would not need to do anything specific for it tc qualify as a PET. Provided the beneficial interest in th property/share of the property was transferred to you children/family it would be a PET.

Note that this assumes you do not retain any interest in the part c the property that is transferred. If you for example transferred share in the property then continued to occupy it or if you receive the rental income this would be classed as a gift with reservation c benefit ('GROB') and as such the value transferred to yo children/family would remain within your estate (unless you paid market rental for your occupation). So a direct gift can clearly l effective in taking the BTL properties out of your estate after years, however the two main drawbacks with a transfer of t properties to your children/family are:

Firstly - The transfer to your children is a disposal for capital gai tax ('CGT') purposes. As you are classed as connected parties the disposal consideration is deemed to be the market value of the properties. You would therefore crystallise a capital gain based on the uplift in market value since the date you acquired it.

If they have been your main residence at any point you could qualify for PPR relief to further reduce the gain. The remaining gain after the annual exemptions (worth around £22,000 for the two of you) would then be charged at 18% or 28% (depending your other income/gains).

If the properties have reduced in value in the current market the gain may not be significant depending on when you did purchase.

Secondly - The other problem is that your children/family would hold the properties at the current market value. On a future disposal by them they would be subject to CGT (assuming they're not occupied as their main residence). On the assumption that property prices will begin to rise again, they could be taxed on a significant uplift in value on a future disposal. By contrast, if the properties are left to them via the will, they would hold at the probate value (ie the market value at death). This would then substantially reduce the CGT charge on a future disposal. The downside of course would be IHT.

The other ancillary problem is that once you've transferred the property, in order to avoid the gift with reservation of benefit provisions, you would not be able to obtain a benefit from the rental income. This would, therefore, be received by (and taxed on) your children/family who now own the property.

Releasing cash as debt

Another option could be to raise debt on the property and gift this to the children rather than actually gifting the property. This could have a number of advantages:

This would be a PET and exempt after 7 years as above. The debt would however still reduce the value for IHT purposes.

Therefore the net effect of this would be similar to a transfer of the actual property and there could be an IHT exemption after 7 years.

2) There would be no CGT charge on the transfer of cash to your children/family as cash is not a chargeable asset. This would therefore be much more attractive than a transfer of the actual property as you'd be able to avoid any tax charge on transfer.

3) You would continue to own the property. You could then leave it to your children/family in your will so that they would inherit at the then market value. The debt secured against the property would reduce it's value for IHT purposes. This would therefore reduce the future capital gain on a disposal by your children/family members.

4) As you're the legal owner of the property you would retain the rental income in your name.

However, the interest on the debt may be able to be claimed as an income tax deduction when calculating the rental profits. This is on the basis that the debt is a withdrawal of capital from the renta business (and there is no overdrawn capital account). We look a this in another chapter.

By raising debt against a BTL property and gifting this, you coul therefore see a number of tax advantages. Not only will any CG charge be avoided but you could still get the IHT benefits and ther could also be an income tax benefit.

22. QUALIFYING FOR INHERITANCE TAX RELIEF ON HOLIDAY LET PROPERTIES

Establishing that a trade exists can be highly advantageous when it comes to minimising your UK taxes. The income tax treatment of rental income, is very similar to trading income (as letting income is treated like trading income for the purposes of calculating tax deductions).

However, there are a number of exemptions and reliefs available to reduce any capital gains tax on a disposal or inheritance tax charges on your death, which only apply to trading businesses.

One of the key benefits of trading status is that it can reduce the rate of capital gains tax to 10%. For anyone looking at selling property an effective 10% rate of tax would be highly attractive.

Some of the other benefits of holding properties for trading purposes rather than investment purposes include:

- Gift relief is available to reduce CGT where properties are used for trading purposes. Again, properties held as stock won't qualify but shares in property trading companies or properties let for trading purposes will qualify. This relief can defer any CGT where shares or properties are transferred at undervalue (eg gifted). This may occur on the passing of a family property business to children. HMRC could look to restrict salary deductions payable by an investment company. In practice they wouldn't look to do this for a trading company.

- Trading income constitutes earnings for the purposes of making tax privileged pension contributions. Under the new pension rules you can make a 'qualifying' pension contribution of up to 100% of your earnings subject to various limits. Rental income would not be classed as earnings for pension purposes.

• Trading properties or shares in a trading company can qualify f an IHT exemptions known as 'business property relief'. The effe of this is to completely eliminate the trading assets shares from individuals estate.

This is highly attractive as the tax saving is potentially 40% of t net asset value.

Qualifying for the Inheritance tax relief

The specific reliefs for capital gains tax (such as rollover relief a entrepreneurs' relief) apply, provided that the property is availab for letting and actually let for specific periods of the year.

For inheritance tax, however, there are no such reliefs. If you wa your holiday cottage to qualify for tax exemption (100% busine property relief) on your death, then you have to be able demonstrate that you have been running the cottage as a busine and not just as a landlord.

What do I have to do to keep on the right side of the taxman?

If you want to be able to claim inheritance tax relief on a holid cottage, you must have done much more than carry out repairs a decoration, take bookings, and greet the guests. Any landlo would do those things.

Any, and preferably all, of the following will be very helpful your case:

* you do all the laundry and provide clean sheets;

* you make up the beds every day;

* you provide telephone and television;

* you give the guests advice on places to visit and local activities

* you provide some form of catering.

It may not be possible for you to deal with the provision of catering, but if you can it is enormously helpful in any discussion with the Revenue. Even if you do not offer any meals, you might be able to provide a packed lunch now and then, or at least you may offer to buy a hamper of selected items to have ready for the guests when they arrive, which of course they will pay for.

When you have done all these things, you need to make sure they are reflected in your advertising and in your paperwork so that you can demonstrate you have gone far beyond the work of an ordinary landlord.

23. USING AN OVERSEAS MORTGAGE

If you're buying property overseas as part of an overseas BTL business you may consider using an overseas mortgage.

Tax implications of using an overseas mortgage to purchase overseas property include:

Interest payments

If you're a UK resident, UK domiciliary, you'll be subject to UK income tax on any rental income that is generated when you let the property. However the interest on a foreign loan to purchase the property is potentially deductible for UK income tax purposes. So using an interest only mortgage to finance your overseas investment properties can be highly tax efficient.

One thing you will need to consider is the tax deduction at source rules. As the tax deduction for interest is a topic in itself, we've looked at this in a separate chapter.

Capital gains tax

Using the mortgage will not impact on the gain on the disposal o the property, as this is based on proceeds less cost, but you wi have to consider the foreign exchange provisions in terms of th currency, particularly if there are any repayments. This is becaus repayment of foreign currency can be treated as a CGT disposal.

Where a loan is received in foreign currency, there is a acquisition of that currency for a consideration equal to its sterlin value at that time. A capital gain or allowable loss may then ari on the disposal of that currency, (eg such as where it is used purchase property). When the foreign currency is used to repay t loan, there is then a disposal of that currency for proceeds equal its sterling value on repayment. However from your perspecti the loan itself is a liability, not an asset and as such any loss on the loan incurred by a borrower is not allowable for capital gains tax purposes.

Therefore if you buy overseas property with an overseas currency mortgage, you would be treated as acquiring the overseas currency, and then using this to purchase the overseas property. Note that the base cost of the overseas property would be the sterling equivalent of the purchase cost. Any subsequent disposal proceeds for the property would also be converted to sterling and the gain would be based on the sterling uplift in value from the base cost.

However on the repayment of the loan this is treated as a disposal equivalent to the sterling value. Therefore you could crystallise a capital gain if you make capital repayments of the overseas currency loan. The gain would be calculated as the difference between the sterling value of the repayment and the original sterling base cost of the loan.

In terms of the calculation, it is likely the Revenue would accept the simplified calculation. Under this you would treat all disposals/repayments of the overseas currency in the tax year, as a single disposal. You should compute the gain or loss by reference to the average price of the pool from which the currency derived.

Exemption for overseas property

There is however a capital gains tax exemption for various foreign currency gains. This states that a gain on the disposal of currency acquired by individuals for their personal expenditure outside the UK of themselves and their family is not a capital gain. This includes expenditure on the provision or maintenance of a residence outside the UK.

You may therefore be able to argue that any gain was in any case exempt if you could show that the overseas property was for your personal use. It would then be just the gain on the future disposal of the land/property that would be charged to UK CGT.

There is now also a blanket CGT exemption for gains from foreign currency bank accounts.

Inheritance tax

If you're a UK domiciliary you would be subject to UK inheritance tax on your worldwide estate. This would therefore include the value of the overseas property. However, it is the net value that is taken into account and therefore, if you had an overseas mortgage secured over the property this would reduce it's value for UK inheritance tax purposes.

Non UK domicile status

If you were a non UK domiciliary, you would effectively be exempt from UK tax on the overseas property providing you retained any rental income or proceeds of disposal overseas. In terms of inheritance tax, you would in any event be exempt from tax on the overseas property.

24. MAKING THE MOST OF THE DROP IN PROPERTY PRICES TO RESTRUCTURE PROPERTY INVESTMENTS

If you have investment properties owned by a company, you may be able to take advantage of the decrease in property prices to transfer them to you and reduce your ultimate tax charge on disposal.

Although the corporation tax rate for most small companies is now 20%, the rate of capital gains tax for higher rate taxpayers is 28%.

However, when you take account of the income tax on extraction of any proceeds this would mean an additional 25% or 30.55% tax charge on you personally.

So if you need to extract the proceeds, holding property via a company may not be the best option.

So what can you do about it?

You could of course transfer the property to you directly. In the past the problem with this was that it would crystallise the capital gain in the company. Given the boom in property prices the gain could be significant and there would be no real benefit unless the property was expected to increase further over the coming years.

This has all changed now. Property prices are on the drop and in some cases they are plummeting rapidly. This could therefore be the perfect opportunity to get the property out of the company ownership and into your hands.

How will the transfer work?

As stated above, the transfer from the company to you would be a disposal for CGT purposes. The gain would represent the uplift in value from the acquisition date to the disposal date. Indexation relief would be due on the acquisition cost.

Any gain that is due would be charged at the companies marginal rate of corporation tax.

Of course the plan is that, at the date of transfer the value of the property would have substantially decreased so that the gain would be minimal. What if the gain had reduced below the original cost price?

In this case the company would crystallise a capital loss which would be offset against any capital gains of the current or future years.

In terms of arranging the transfer, the company could either transfer it to you for nil consideration, or you could look to purchase it from the company. In either case, the capital gain in the company would be the same and it would be based on proceeds equivalent to the market value. If the company simply transferred it to you there would be another consideration - income tax.

The amount of any undervalue on the transfer would be classed a a distribution. This is like a dividend and would be subject t income tax on you.

You should therefore carefully consider how the transfer would b structured.

Of course, if there was a directors' loan account ("DLA") balanc remaining you could cover part of the extraction value with thi This would usually be the case where you sold the property to th company and left the proceeds outstanding. Providing this DL has not been fully utilised in the intervening period, it would b available to cover the transfer.

You may even have a case where the DLA exceeds the transf value.

the value at the date of transfer to the company was, say 00,000 (which was left outstanding) and the current value is 50,000, the transfer to you personally could be made which ould use only part of the loan account. The remainder could be ed to extract future profits from the company.

nother option to extract from the company free of income tax uld be by becoming non UK resident. In this case you could tentially be outside the scope of UK income tax on distributions.

ere is a problem though if there is a significant drop in the value the property, below the original transfer value. In this case if the operty was retained in the company, the base cost would be gher. You'd therefore need to take account of all of the taxes to sess whether there could be significant tax savings. The problem that a capital loss in the company may not be offset unless there e future capital gains, even though you are charged on the gain rsonally.

ample

transfers a property to B Limited at a value of £1,000,000. The lue drops to £700,000 and he then transfers it back to himself. e company would have a capital loss of £300,000.

disposal of the property for £1.2M would crystallise a capital in of £500,000. The CGT on this if owned personally would be 40,000 (assuming higher rate taxpayers). If the property was ained in the company ownership the gain would have been 00,000. The corporation tax on this (assuming the company paid rporation tax at the small company rate) would be around 0,000 (based on a small company rate of 20%). Provided there s a limited extraction of cash from the company (or the areholder was non resident), owning personally would increase e immediate CGT charge.

hilst there is a £140,000 tax charge on the individual compared £40,000 in the company, in the individual scenario there is also a capital loss of £300,000 in the company. Providing the company could utilise this loss, overall the transfer may still however be justified.

If not, as will be the case for many companies, this technique works best when the current property value equates to the original transfer value (ie no gain on transfer and the gain will effectively all be charged on you personally on a future disposal).

25. USING A HOLDING COMPANY FOR PROPERTY INVESTMENTS

Ensuring that you have the correct structure set up for your property investment or property development activities, can be half the battle in terms of minimising taxes.

Many property developers hold property developments via separate companies.

Whilst this can be attractive in terms of limiting the liabilities, you need to look carefully at the tax implications.

In particular there's a big difference between

- An individual owning the two property investment companies personally. In other words he owns 100% of the shares in A and 100% of the shares in B, and
- The same individual owning 100% of the shares in X Limited. This then owned 100% of the shares in Company A and Company B.

Why use a holding company?

Many property investors structure their property investment activities as in the first example. Aside from the issue of whether a corporate structure is the best option for property investors, if they do opt for a corporate structure the first structure can have some significant disadvantages - particularly if one of the companies realises a capital loss (perhaps more likely given the current economic slowdown).

In order to transfer assets between the companies tax efficiently they would need to form a group for capital gains tax purposes. This effectively means that a company forms a group with its 75% subsidiaries and 75% subsidiaries of those subsidiaries, and so on.

It is also required that there is at least an effective 51% ownership.

Therefore if both A & B were owned under a holding company such as X Ltd (with the shares owned by you), this would form a group.

The key benefit of a group for capital gains tax purposes is that it can transfer an asset with a latent loss tax free to a company with a capital gain, and then crystallise the loss in the gain company. Provided the gain crystallises in the same accounting period as the loss, or in a later accounting period to which the loss is carried forward, the tax charge is only on the net gain, if any.

If there is no capital gains group there would be no option to offset losses between the two companies. So you could have a situation where Company A may realise a loss, and Company B a gain on a disposal. In this case the loss from Company A couldn't be offset against the gain in Company B.

If there was a group the loss could be used.

The group structure also allows the transfer of any rental losse between the two companies which would not apply if there was n group.

Disadvantages of using a holding company

There are though some disadvantages to using the group structure.

In particular:

•There will be an extra company for the purposes of the associate company rules. As such, dependent on the level of profits in ea company, it could push one or more of the companies into the ne corporation tax band. Of course this depends completely on t level of profits and may have no impact whatever.

• If the companies are owned directly by the shareholder, there always the option of selling the shares in the company rather th e underlying property. This would then be taxed at 18%or 28% ı the individual (or even exempt if the shareholder was non UK sident).

ıe holding company could sell the shares in the underlying ›mpany, but this would crystallise a capital gain in the holding ›mpany. If the subsidiary was an investment company the ıbstantial shareholding exemption would not be available.

ıis may not be an issue though if a sale of the shares was not on e cards.

 this case the proceeds would be transferred free of tax to the ›lding company, and could be extracted by the shareholder with e same tax implications as if he held the company directly.

26. SAVING INHERITANCE TAX ON INVESTMENT PROPERTY BY USING A TRUST

With rates of inheritance tax at 40%, this can represent a huge chunk of your wealth that goes to the taxman. Anyone with a substantial estate will therefore be looking at opportunities to reduce the potential inheritance tax charge in the future.

Given the boom in house prices over the last 10 years or so, property investors could be looking at huge inheritance tax liabilities. OK, the amount of any mortgage is deducted before inheritance tax is charged, but nevertheless with the increases in value the net estate could be huge.

One of the problems for anyone with investment property who is also looking to reduce inheritance tax, is that simply gifting the properties to children or grandchildren will in many cases not be tax efficient. Although from an inheritance perspective, it will be excluded from their estate after 7 years, the transfer would also be a disposal for capital gains tax purposes.

For capital gains tax, any mortgages are excluded and the gain wil essentially represent the uplift in value. Of course, the capital gain tax rate is now 18% or 28% and the tax charge could b substantial. One option to 'have your cake and eat it' is to use property investment trust.

The trust could be established as a discretionary trust or even a interest in possession trust. In both cases they would still b 'relevant property trusts'.

Relevant property trusts are treated as a separate entity to th settlor (ie the person who makes the transfer), and therefo property held within such a trust will usually be excluded from th settlor's estate for inheritance tax purposes. The two provisos he are:

• they still need to survive for at least seven years from the date of the transfer.
•the settlor and his wife need to ensure that they don't retain the right to benefit from the trust. If they do, anti avoidance rules (known as the reservation of benefit provisions) can apply to treat the property transferred as part of the settlor's estate

What about capital gains tax?

The transfer to the trust is still a disposal for capital gains tax purposes, however it's possible to holdover the capital gain on the transfer. The trustees can also holdover the gain if they transfer the property to a trust beneficiary in the future. Effectively this means that the eventual beneficiary will hold the property at the same cost that the settlor had.

To claim holdover relief though, it's important that the settlor, their spouse and any minor children can't benefit from the trust. You'll therefore need to make the trust for the benefit of:

Uncles
Adult children
Grandchildren
Brothers
Sisters
Aunts
Nephews
Nieces
Cousins
Separated couples
Divorced couples
Relatives of your partner you are living with (if you're not married or in a civil partnership with your partner)
Relatives of divorced parties

It's also worth noting that you can't use this and also claim principal private residence ('PPR') relief. So, you couldn't transfer a property to a trust for the benefit of your adult children, claim holdover relief to defer the gain and also have the trustees claiming PPR relief on the basis it was his main residence.

Downsides

This all sounds pretty good. Transfer investment property to a trust for adult children or grandchildren. Defer any gain and avoid IHT after 7 years.

It is good…but the downside is that the trust itself is subject to a separate inheritance tax regime. This can get very complicated however essentially there are 3 key points when inheritance tax can be an issue:

•On the transfer to the trust
•After 10 years
•On the transfer of properties out of the trust

Nevertheless, there is good way to minimise the effect of the provisions. This relies on using the inheritance tax nil rate band. This is currently £325,000. Assuming no other transfers in the previous 7 years you could transfer a property to the trust with a value of up to this amount free of any inheritance tax to the trust.

If, as many people do, properties are owned jointly this means you could transfer a value of up to £650,000 to the trust. In fact when you take into account the annual inheritance tax exemption it wi be slightly more than this. Each person has a £3,000 annua exemption that is deducted from gifts before inheritance tax taken into account. As a bonus this can be carried forward for year.

This means that as a couple you could transfer a property with value of up to £662,000 into the trust tax free. This could easi represent a couple of properties and represents a CGT free transf It would also be free of inheritance tax after seven years.

This could then be repeated seven years later to take account of t new 'untouched' inheritance tax threshold. Assuming this was £400,000, you could transfer £812,000 as a couple. Over the course of 20 years or so this would easily allow £2,000,000 worth of properties to be transferred out of the estate. This would save inheritance tax of £800,000 and also be free from capital gains tax.

This £800,000 inheritance tax saving is not a complete picture though. The trust would also need to consider it's own position. It will be subject to an inheritance tax charge on the value of the trust assets every 10 years.

The extent of any inheritance tax charge would depend on the value of the trust asset as well as the nil rate band at that point.

If we assume that a couple transferred property worth £662,000 into a trust, and then 7 years later transferred property worth a further £812,000 into the trust the cost of the trust assets would be £1.474M. Assuming that these properties have now grown to £2,000,000.

The nil rate band may be £500,000.

The 10 year tax charge in the trust is calculated as:

Trust Assets £2,000,000 Nil rate bands -£1,000,000 Chargeable amount in the trust = £1,000,000

IHT charge at 20% = £200,000.

ffective rate = £200,000/£2,000,000*3/10 = 3%.

here is then a reduction in this for each calendar quarter that the roperties were in the trust.

herefore the property in the trust originally would be taxed at 3% d the property transferred in after 7 years would be charged at 1%. The inheritance tax charge could therefore be in the region £50,000.

Although not an insignificant amount, when compared to the value of the assets in the trust (£2,000,000) and the potential IHT charge if held personally (£800,000) it represents a considerable inheritance tax saving.

27. SHOULD YOU USE A COMPANY FOR PROPERTY INVESTMENTS?

It's a pretty common question, and is something that should be considered well before you actually buy any property (or even exchange contracts). Note that what we're mainly considering here is the case where someone is buying property to either renovate and sell on or to hold as a buy to let.

If you're just buying property that you will occupy as your main residence, you should almost always buy it in your own name. Why? Well if you're occupying it as your main residence you'll be able to obtain principal private residence ('PPR') relief on a future disposal, which will ensure that any profit you make on the disposal is free of tax.

Aside from this one of the key issues will be whether you would intend to sell developed properties or retain them long term to generate capital growth and rental returns.

In either case the initial consideration will be whether to hold the property via a company or personally. You should generally avoid 'mixing' these. For example, one possible option would be to buy property personally, develop it and then transfer it to a wholly owned limited company which would rent the property out.

This should generally be avoided. If you hold the property in your name, develop it and then transfer to a company, the transfer would be a chargeable disposal for income tax/capital gains tax purposes. The market value of the properties would be likely to be used and any profit/gain would be likely to be taxed on you personally. This could be the case even though the property would then be held by the company long term.

Therefore, ideally, you would look to establish the correct structure for holding the property from the outset, and either hold personally or transfer the property pre development to the company.

If you were looking to develop properties, any profits would be assessed to income tax. On this basis, and assuming you would be retaining most of the profits within the business, with minimal extractions (ie retaining cash in the business for future use) it would be likely to be more tax efficient to use a company to conduct the trade.

If you carried out the trade personally, you would be taxed at 20%/40%/45% on the profits generated when you sold each property. If the profits were significant this would be predominantly at the 40% or 45% rate of income tax. This would apply irrespective of whether the proceeds was reinvested into further development properties or not. In addition you could be subject to NIC, at a rate of 9% up to the higher rate tax band, and 2% on additional profits.

By contrast, if you were to use a company, the company could earn profits of up to £300,000 pa and pay corporation tax at 20%.

It's worthwhile noting that if you own any other companies thi £300,000 limit is reduced according to the number of companies For example if you owned one other company the 20% tax banc would be reduced to £150,000.

In this case, if annual profits would be above this, it may b worthwhile to consider simply carrying out both trades from on company, particularly if the profits of one of the companies is ver low. This would then increase the 20% tax band to £300,000.

The company would not be charged to NIC on the profits but a the company is a separate legal entity, you would need to extrac cash from the company. If you had provided funds to the compan as a loan on the start up you could extract amounts up to this fr of income tax and NIC. You could also consider taking cash as dividend to utilise any basic rate tax band, again effectively free income tax.

If you were looking to retain properties long term and benefit from capital growth and rental income, keeping them in your name would likely be preferable. In this case you would be classed as a property investor rather than a property trader and the reliefs under CGT for personal as opposed to company ownership would be greater. In addition the tax rate for private investors is now set at 18% or 28% (depending on whether you are a higher rate taxpayer or not).

This means that personal ownership will lead to a tax increase of around 8% for most people however this ignores the fact that company owners need to get the profits out of the company. Extracting profits is subject to income tax (at 25% if within the higher rate tax band).

It's also worth bearing in mind that if the gain on disposal exceeded £300,000 the company would then pay tax at a marginal rate of 25% on the gain above £300,000.

Individual owners also have the annual CGT exemptions to offset which are currently £11,000 each. So if you owned with your spouse that's an extra tax deduction of £22,000. A company is only entitled to relief for inflation.

f you used a company to hold investment properties, the gains on . future disposal would be higher, and you would then have the roblem of extracting the large disposal proceeds (unless the roceeds were retained in the company).

his assumes that the key consideration would be capital growth. .s an investor you would also obtain rental income, which would e likely to be taxed at 20%/40%/45%. In any case, if the roperties are highly geared, any rental profits would be unlikely be significant after the mortgage interest was deducted.

herefore when considering whether to purchase via a company or rsonally as a first step you should ensure that you carefully nsider the nature of your property activities and whether they ill be classed as trading or investment.

It should also be borne in mind that there are a package of specific tax measures aimed at companies that hold property via either a UK or offshore company. Where the property is valued at more than £2Million there can be an annual tax charge and in addition the SDLT cost on purchase will be 15%.

The £2Million threshold means it won't affect many investors.

However in the 2014 Budget it was announced that this will be reduced to £1Million from 2015 and £500,000 from 2016.

This could potentially catch a lot more people who hold property via a company.

There are however a number of specific reliefs for property investors.

The key property reliefs are:

a. Property development businesses - dwellings held for the purpose of the property development trade of the company and no occupied at any time by a "connected person";

b. Property rental businesses - dwellings held for the purpose o letting to third parties for rent on a commercial basis and nc occupied at any time by a "connected person"; and

c. Property trading businesses - dwellings held for the purpose of trade of buying and selling property and not occupied at any tim by a "connected person".

The legislation states that:

"...Property rental business means a business that is a proper business for the purposes of the CTA 2009 (but see subsection (3

(5) Qualifying property rental business means a property rent business that is carried

(a) on a commercial basis, and

(b) with a view to the realisation of profits..."

Therefore for most companies that are classed as carrying on a rental business and assuming the property was not let to a connected person and charged a market rent it is likely that the relief from these rules would apply. You can see more on these rules in Chapter 29.

28. BUYING PROPERTY WITH A GIFTED DEPOSIT

Investors will often structure these arrangement by doing deals with builders in various 'no money down scenarios'. Typically these could be done in various ways such as:

The builder has gifted the deposit (typically 15%) (for example purchase price and contract price £100,000, deposit paid by builder £15,000, mortgage £85,000. Stamp Duty is paid on the £100,000.)

The builder has paid a cashback after the completion ie purchase price £100,000, purchaser pays the £15,000 deposit and obtains a mortgage of £85,000. After the completion the builder then pays the purchaser £5,000. Stamp Duty is again paid on the £100,000 purchase price.

The question arises how these cash backs and gifted deposits are treated for UK tax purposes?

In the case of a cashback, a Revenue Statement of Practice state that 'the cash back is not a capital sum derived from an asset and a such is not chargeable to CGT in the purchasers hands'. Althoug it could exceptionally be classed as trading income, on the basi that the purchaser is a property trader it would be unlikely to fa within the rental income rules and as such it should not be subje to income tax.

In terms of CGT, if the purchase documentation specifically stat that on completion there would be a cash back, the future base co for CGT purposes should be regarded as the net cost (ie after t cashback has been deducted). This will therefore increase the ga on a future disposal of the property by £15,000 in the abo example.

In terms of the gifted deposit, again there should be no t

implications on the purchase. Essentially, the vendor has given the purchaser a discount , and as such the reduction should not be subject to income tax or CGT.

As the purchasers base cost for a future disposal is restricted to the amount of the consideration in money or money's worth given for acquiring the asset (ie the amount actually expended by the purchaser) again the future base cost would be the net cost, after the deduction of the gifted deposit.

There are cases though where it may be possible to argue that in the gifted deposit scenario the cost for CGT purposes would be the cost ignoring the gifted deposit.

This may work as follows:

Mr A is buying a property from an old couple that occupy the house as their main residence. It is realistically and genuinely worth £100,000, but Mr A has been able to buy it for £80,000, as the old couple are giving it to him cheap because he's a friend of their sons.

Mr A has secured an 85% BTL mortgage on this for £68,000 and the remaining £12,000 he's putting in himself. Being a particularly smart investor, Mr A has the the contract amended to £100,000, with £20,000 of this being classed as a gifted deposit. His thinking here is that when he sells the property in the future, he'll have a CGT base cost of £100,000 which could save him extra CGT of £8,000 as opposed to the £80,000 base cost. The vendor may not be concerned as if it's their main residence, they'd be exempt from CGT in any case.

How would this be viewed in tax terms?

Mr A may be able to argue that the acquisition cost of the property for CGT purposes would be the £100,000 as opposed to £80,000.

Under normal circumstances, the disposal proceeds for the vendor along with the corresponding acquisition cost to the purchaser would be the actual proceeds received for the property (ie £80,000) as stated above.

However, there are broadly two circumstances when the market value of the property would replace the actual disposal. The first is where the transaction is between connected parties. This would apply to transfers between family members and business partners, and would not be relevant in this situation.

Secondly, the market value is used when the disposal is not a bargain made at arms length.

A bargain made at arm's length is a normal commercial transaction between two or more persons. All of the parties involved will be trying to obtain the best deal for themselves in their particular circumstances. This would apply to the builder making a gifted deposit in the above example, but this case is subtly different.

A transaction is `otherwise than by way of a bargain made at arm's length' when one of the persons involved in the transaction does not intend to get the best deal for themselves and that person enters into the transaction with the subjective intention of giving some gratuitous benefit to the other person. The typical example of this is a gift of an asset.

Therefore in relation to the this scenario, it would need to b considered whether the market value rule could apply.

As it is currently structured it could be argued that there was n bargain at arms length, however I would expect that this could b denied by HMRC dependent on the circumstances. The vendor may for example be letting Mr A have the property for less, for quick sale (eg if they couldn't sell) and this would therefore still b an arms length transaction.

If however, they were to accept £80,000 for the property and gi the remaining £20,000, this should ensure that their disposal valu is £100,000 (ie market value) and Mr A's acquisition cost is als £100,000. This is on the basis that there is no bargain at arn length and in this case the old couple are subjectively letting Mr A have the property cheaply without intending to get the best price for themselves. Note that the £100,000 cost would apply for CGT purposes and this structure would only work as Mr A is acquiring the property at less than market value.

Therefore a deed of gift would need to be drafted identifying the gift. Mr A would need to discuss the impact on the conveyancing/mortgage with the solicitor/mortgage company.

Essentially the deed of gift would ensure that the cost/proceeds are uplifted for CGT purposes.. From the vendors perspective providing the property is their main residence, and has been throughout their period of ownership, they should be entitled to full principal private residence ('PPR') to eliminate any gain on disposal. If the property was not their main residence, their gain would be calculated on the market value of the property and as such would increase their CGT charge.

Note that in terms of inheritance tax, the vendors would be treated as making a gift of £20,000. This would be a 'potentially exempt transfer' ('PET') and they would need to survive for at least seven years in order for the £20,000 gift to be excluded from their estates for Inheritance tax purposes. Of course, if their estates are below the IHT nil rate band this may not be an issue, however, if they have a substantial estate the additional tax (in this case potentially £8,000) would be borne by their estate.

29. BUYING UK PROPERTY AS A NON-RESIDENT

It is useful to consolidate some of the issues covered in previous chapters and consider a typical scenario, where a UK non-resident and non-domiciled individual wishes to purchase a UK property.

Jack is resident and domiciled in Spain. He has relatives in the UK and is interested in purchasing a property here because (a) he wants somewhere to stay when he visits and (b) he has heard that UK property prices are set to rise.

The question is ... how from a tax perspective should he structure the purchase?

There are broadly two ways to buy the property:

- By using direct ownership, or
- Using some form of intermediary like a trust or company.

This chapter is based on the 2014/2015 tax year. We look a potential changes from April 2015 at the end of this chapter.

DIRECT OWNERSHIP

Capital Gains Tax

From a capital gains tax perspective direct ownership is potentiall attractive:

- The Principal Private Residence (PPR) relief operates to exem a gain on the disposal of an individual's main residence. Even if t property is not, in fact, Jack's main residence, he could certain submit an election to have it treated as his main residence.

- As he is non-resident, he would not in any case be liable

UK capital gains tax on the disposal of any assets.

Inheritance Tax

The inheritance tax position is, however, not as good. The holding of property in the UK would mean that Jack has a UK estate and, as well as probate being required on his death, the house would be subject to inheritance tax to the extent that the value exceeds the £325,000 nil rate band. As the value of the property is expected to rise rapidly, this could result in a significant tax bill were he to die while still owning the asset.

There are, however, a number of methods available to Jack to reduce or eliminate any inheritance tax charge:

Use of Multiple Ownership

The property could be acquired in multiple ownership. For example, Jack, his wife and children could all own the property jointly.

Provided the individuals have no other UK assets, it is likely that each share will be below the nil rate band.

In order to avoid problems with the 'gift with reservation of benefit' legislation, it is necessary to gift cash to the family members, which they can then use to purchase their shares of the property.

The gift, with reservation of benefit (GROB) provisions, applies to property in particular, where an interest in a property is given away, yet the person gifting the interest still continues to reside in the property. For inheritance tax purposes, the whole value of the property is still regarded as included in the occupier's estate for inheritance tax purposes.

Gifting of Property

Another solution would be to gift cash to a younger member of the family who can then make the acquisition. The gift will be exempt from inheritance tax, provided the person making the gift survives seven years. The above GROB rules would not apply as the gift was a cash gift.

The UK pre-owned assets tax charge should also not be relevant if Jack is non-UK resident.

The property will then belong to the donee (the younger family member) and if the donee were to die, it would be included in his estate for inheritance tax purposes.

Mortgages

The value of an individual's estate is essentially the market value of the assets at the date of death, less any liabilities outstanding a the date of death.

It is therefore possible to effectively reduce any inheritance ta charge to zero by obtaining a substantial loan against the value o the property.

Provided the mortgage reduces the 'net value' of the property t below the nil rate band (currently £325,000), there will be n inheritance tax payable.

The mortgage funds obtained can be invested overseas and an interest return would then be exempt from UK income ta provided the interest income is not remitted to the UK.

USING A TRUST TO OWN THE PROPERTY

Capital Gains Tax

The Principal Private Residence relief is extended to situatio where a beneficiary is entitled to occupy a house under the terr of a trust deed. In these circumstances, the trustees would be al to claim PPR relief when they sell the property.

In the case of a non-UK domiciliary, as the trustees are non-resident they would not, in any case, be liable to UK capital gains tax.

It would only be if the settlor of the trust (or his close family) were also a beneficiary and became UK resident that the gains of the trust could be attributed to him under the anti-avoidance provisions.

Inheritance Tax

The trust will be subject to special inheritance tax rules. One of the key implications is that it could be subject to an inheritance tax charge every 10 years starting with the date of commencement.

USING AN OFFSHORE COMPANY

The property could be owned by a non-resident company. In this case the non-domiciliary would own the shares in the company.

As the shares are non-UK property, they would be exempt from inheritance tax. The key risks are:

The company's residence position may be closely scrutinised by the taxman, and it may be difficult to show that the central management and control is exercised outside the UK, particularly if all directors are UK resident and the asset of the company is a UK property. If HMRC is able to successfully argue that the company is UK resident, any gain on the disposal of the property would be subject to UK corporation tax and no PPR relief would be available.

If the property is valued at more than £2Million the offshore company itself may be subject to UK CGT – we look at this shortly.

In addition, on a disposal of the shares in the company, no capital gains tax would be payable by Jack provided he remained non-resident. If he were UK resident, he may not be charged to UK CGT provided the proceeds were retained outside the UK and he were subject to the remittance basis, as he's a non-UK domiciliary.

TAX PLANNING FOR NON-RESIDENTS OWNING UK PROPERTY INVESTMENT COMPANIES

Many individuals hold their UK properties in a UK company.

When these individuals move overseas and lose UK residence, they will often hold onto their property company.

The company has to pay UK corporation tax on any rental profits. However, the shareholder can potentially extract the remaining profits free of UK income tax/withholding tax and can always sell the shares in the company free of capital gains tax.

If the company sells the properties, however, corporation tax will have to be paid on the capital gains.

One important issue is financing the properties. This could come from either the UK or overseas.

UK financing is often preferred. The UK company would obtain a corporation tax deduction for the interest, but the shareholder could then extract the funds which could be invested overseas free of UK income tax. If the shareholder is resident in a tax haven, it may be possible to completely avoid income tax on the interest generated. This is potentially a win-win scenario with the interest being tax deductible in the UK company and reinvested overseas free of tax.

If financing is obtained from overseas the risk is that the tax deduction at source rules could apply. These can require tax to be deducted by the payer where the interest is from a UK source but the payment is made overseas. In the case of a UK company paying interest overseas, the net result is that the UK company may need to account for 20% income tax on the interest paid overseas.

The key issue is where the 'source' of the interest is. Revenue and Customs would look at a number of factors to determine whether the interest has a UK source:

- The residence of the debtor (this is usually taken to be the place where the debt will be enforced),
- The source from which interest is paid,
- Where the interest is paid, and
- The nature and location of any security for the debt.

If the loan were made to a UK company from overseas and in respect of UK property, it would be likely that the interest would have a UK source and as such be subject to the deduction of tax at source rules. Therefore whilst it would be deductible for the UK company when calculating its taxable profits, there could be a 20% income tax liability on the interest.

The options to avoid this are limited if the interest is paid overseas. A payment to a UK bank avoids these issues.

The main option to reduce withholding tax on interest paid overseas would be to rely on a double tax treaty. These provide for an exemption or reduction in UK tax deducted at source depending on the particular agreement that the UK has with the country in question. You could therefore ensure that the deduction at source from the UK was eliminated.

Transferring Properties to an Offshore Company

Another option would be to transfer the properties to an offshore ompany. The main tax issue here would have to pay corporation x on any capital gain made up to the date of transfer.

o, this strategy works best if there has only been a nominal crease in the value of the properties.

transfer overseas could, however, shelter you from paying tax on y future gains. If the properties remain in a UK company, any increase in value will be subject to UK corporation tax at a rate of up to 21% from April 2014.

If the properties are held by a non-resident, UK tax on the gain could be avoided. The rental income would fall within the non-resident landlord scheme and an application would need to be made to receive the interest gross (without UK income tax deducted on the rental income).

Income tax (note not corporation tax) would be assessed via a self-assessment return. Any interest paid to a non-resident lender could still be claimed as a tax deduction in calculating the UK taxable profits.

Another benefit of holding the properties via a non UK company would be if the shareholder has lost UK domicile. A non UK domiciliary would be subject to UK inheritance tax on the value of the UK shares if it were not a trading company.

By contrast a non domiciliary wouldn't be subject to inheritanc tax on the value of overseas shares if the UK properties were helc via an offshore company.

2013 Changes

In order to tackle the so called enveloping of high value propertie into companies, the Government has adopted a threefold approach

- with effect from 21 March 2012 a new 15% rate of stamp dut land tax (SDLT) applies on purchases of UK residential propertie worth over £2 million by non-natural persons;
- from 1 April 2013 an annual charge will apply to U residential properties valued at over £2 million owned by no natural persons; and
- from 6 April 2013 the CGT regime will be extended to gai on the disposal of UK residential property, and shares or interes in such property, by non-natural persons who are non-UK reside or UK resident.

The aim is to discourage enveloping of property and all three proposals will run in tandem.

Any new purchases of properties worth more than £2 million by an offshore company will suffer a 15% SDLT charge on the purchase. The annual charge based on value will then be payable going forward and, disposals of the property will now be subject to CGT.

Non Natural Persons

The proposals don't just apply to "offshore companies". They include all "non-natural persons" which encompasses companies, collective investment schemes and partnerships in which a non-natural person is a partner.

However, the 15% charge will not apply to the purchase of a property by a trust even though one or more of the trustees is a company.

Annual Charge

An annual charge will come into effect on 1 April 2013 and will be payable at the start of the period of account, i.e., by 15 April of each year. It is proposed that the charge will operate on a pro rata basis so that if the property is sold during the year, a repayment of part of the charge can be claimed.

A return will be required each year for each relevant dwelling within the charge owned by the non-natural person.

The return must include information on the property:

Its address, Land Registry title, details of the 'beneficial owners' of the property and their address if different from the property address.

The levels of the annual charge will be set at:

- £15,000 pa for properties valued at between £2 - 5 million;
- £35,000 for properties valued at between £5 - 10 million;
- £70,000 for properties valued at between £10 - 20 million;
- £140,000 for properties worth more than £20 million.

Introducing an annual charge on capital values means that the UK now has its first form of wealth tax (a form of tax found in many European jurisdictions including France and Spain).

New CGT charge

The new charge to capital gains tax will not apply to trustees (although they may be subject to tax under other, existing provisions). However, contrary to the Treasury's previous announcements, the charge will apply to both UK resident and non-UK resident non-natural persons.

The charge will only apply to "ATED-related gains": The ATED related gains are essentially the gains from 6 April 2013 or the day of acquisition (if later).

If, for part of the period of ownership, the property was exemp from the Annual Charge, there is a reduction in the amount of gai subject to the capital gains tax charge to reflect this period c exemption.

In addition, where a UK resident non-natural person disposes of property held pre-6 April 2013, the gains arising on a disposal wi be split between pre-6 April 2013 gains and from 6 April 201 gains. The gains treated as arising pre-6 April 2013 gains will b charged to corporation tax, if applicable, while gains from 6 Apr 2013 will be subject to capital gains tax.

A seller may elect to be charged to capital gains tax instead for t whole gain and must make an election on their tax return if th wish to do so.

ATED-related gains will not be attributed to shareholders in offshore close companies.

There are complex provisions regarding the use of any losses realised from the sale of high-value UK residential property.

In essence, losses can only be used to offset future gains arising from the sale of high-value UK residential property.

There are also provisions that deem a minimum consideration of £2 million on sale when calculating the loss available.

The rate of tax, and latent gains

The CGT charge will only apply to disposals of residential property where the amount of the consideration for the disposal exceeds £2 million.

As stated above, there is to be 'grandfathering' (i.e., protection for) latent gains that have accrued but not been realised before the extension of the CGT regime.

Although the property market as a whole has seen prices fall or emain static in recent years, those at the higher end of the market have seen large increases and substantial gains could have been built up where properties have been held for a longer period of time.

The rate of CGT will be 28%.

Meaning of 'residential property'

The definition of residential property for these purposes will ollow the meaning of 'dwelling' used for the 15% SDLT rate and he new annual charge.

The CGT regime will apply to disposals of residential property in eveloped structures irrespective of the use to which it is put. For xample, it will apply to commercially let residential property.

What to do if you are caught by the new anti avoidance rules?

There are a couple of options that could be considered:

De-enveloping

One option is to remove the property from the ownership of the company and move it into personal ownership.

As a result of this new legislation, many people holding such property through BVI companies are thinking about "de-enveloping".

In most cases, the de-enveloping process will be carried out by

(i) placing the BVI (or other offshore) company into voluntary liquidation and then

(ii) distributing in specie the affected property holdings.

This avoids the new punitive tax regime, but it clearly exposes the ultimate beneficial owner (if a non-dom) to UK Inheritance Tax and results in the loss of confidentiality which they previously enjoyed. CGT may also be a determining factor in whether this is a viable option. There might also be other issues if the non-dom is resident in the UK.

Offshore trust structure

For many non-doms a preferable approach may be to convert the offshore company holding structure to an offshore trust holding structure.

Corporate trustees are exempt from the above taxes and for most people transferring property already owned by an offshore company to an offshore trust may be the most cost effective way forward.

Where an offshore trust structure is already in place, with trustees holding a BVI company which in turn holds UK property, it might be advantageous to de-envelope the UK property (by liquidating the BVI company) so that the property is then held directly by the trustees.

Alternatively, if the BVI company is held directly by a non-dom, he or she may consider transferring the shares into an offshore trust now shortly before the BVI company is liquidated, with the same end result of the property then being held directly by trustees.

If the trustees are individuals, they should retire in favour of corporate trustees, so the tax exemptions can be enjoyed.

Budget 2014 changes

They will reduce the £2,000,000 threshold to £500,000.

There will now be three "bands" that can be affected by these "ATED" provisions:

- Properties valued between £500K - £1Million
- Properties valued between £1Million - £2Million
- Properties valued over £2Million

he existing reliefs and exemptions will apply.

low the new rules will apply

roperties valued between £500K - £1Million

TED - This will apply from 1 April 2016 and there will be an nual charge of £3,500 payable by the company.

DLT- SDLT at 15% will be paid for all properties purchased via company above £500K on or after 20 March 2014.

GT- The extension to the ATED-related CGT charge will take effect from 6 April 2016 and will apply only to that part of the gain that is accrued on or after that date.

Properties valued between £1Million - £2Million

ATED - This will apply from 1 April 2015 and there will be an annual charge of £7,000 payable by the company.

SDLT- SDLT at 15% will be paid for all properties purchased via a company above above £500K on or after 20 March 2014.

CGT- The extension to the ATED-related CGT charge will take effect from 6 April 2015 and will apply only to that part of the gain that is accrued on or after that date.

Properties valued above £2Million

There will be no changes to these and the existing ATED regime will apply.

CONCLUSION

Deciding how a non-domiciliary should own UK property is clearly not a straightforward decision.

Much will depend on the particular circumstances and your personal preferences. For example, you may be more anxious to avoid capital gains tax than inheritance tax.

To a certain extent the simplest route – direct ownership – offers some important tax advantages provided potential inheritance tax can be avoided in some way, for example, by using debt.

HOW SHOULD YOU PURCHASE UK PROPERTY AS A NON-RESIDENT GIVEN THE 2015 CHANGES?

The proposal to charge non UK residents to UK CGT on disposals of UK residential property will have a significant impact on how such property should be purchased as from April 2015.

It is too early to make definitive decisions, however even at this stage there are quite a few issues to consider.

The key taxes to consider will be income tax, CGT, Inheritance tax and SDLT.

From an income tax perspective, however UK property is owned, income tax will be charged on UK rental profits. This will fall under the non resident landlord scheme with basic rate tax deducted at source (unless a claim is made to receive income gross).

Therefore whether property is owned personally, via a company or via a trust, UK income tax would be charged. You would need to look to other structuring aspects to reduce income tax on rental profits (eg tax efficient financing).

n terms of inheritance tax (IHT), if you are non UK domiciled you would be exempt from UK IHT on foreign assets, but UK assets would be within the scope of UK IHT. You would have the nil rate band to offset but even so the tax could be significant if the property value is substantial.

Again, if you were to hold personally, considering tax efficient financing of the property could be advisable. Debt secured on the property could reduce the value of the property in the estate and reduce any IHT liability.

You could hold via an offshore company. The advantage to this is that it would effectively convert the property value into foreign property for UK IHT purposes (as the property value would then be reflected in the share value).

or non UK domiciliaries this would then take the property value outside of their estate for UK IHT. The downside is that if the property was valued in excess of £2M there would be an annual charge under the ATED provisions. There would also be a CGT charge on disposal as well as a higher SDLT rate (potentially

15%). Note that the £2M limit is reducing to £1,000,000 from 2015 and £500,000 for 2016 for the purposes of CGT and the Annual Charge.

Currently property owned by an offshore company which is valued at less than £2M would not be subject to CGT on disposal. This is the same treatment as where property is owned by a non-resident individual.

Following the 2013 Autumn Statement this may change from April 2015.

We don't know the details and scope of the proposed changes yet but it is likely that non resident individuals holding UK residential property will be subject to CGT on a disposal. It also appears as though there will not be a £2M limit. We don't know whether it will extend to offshore companies holding UK property but would assume that it would. There are therefore still a number of aspects we aren't aware of and which would need to be considered.

In terms of the most advisable structure, it may be that whether the property is owned personally or via an offshore company, UK CGT would apply from April 2015 on a disposal. In any case for properties valued in excess of £500,000 from 2016 a CGT charge would arise. The advantage of the company is that it can avoid IHT but there would then be the ATED provisions to consider.

It may be the case that if the property is less than £500,000 using an offshore company could be beneficial to avoid UK IHT. If the property is more than £500,000 you would need to consider the IHT saving with the annual ATED cost and increased SDLT cost. It could also be attractive to considering keeping the property individual names but looking at other strategies to reduce IHT purchasing in joint ownership and using debt to reduce the taxable value.

The other option is to use a trust to hold the property. An offshore trust would be subject to UK IHT on the value of UK property. wouldn't be classed as excluded property unless an offshore company was used to hold the property which would then bring the same issues as above. Note though that using a trust would bring the UK IHT regime for discretionary trusts into play.

In particular there would be an IHT "anniversary charge" every 10 years although this is at a significantly reduced IHT rate (max 6%). There would also be an IHT charge on trust distributions. Again we don't know details yet but it is likely that the offshore trust would be subject to CGT on disposals of UK residential property after April 2015.

ABOUT THE AUTHOR

Lee Hadnum LLB ACA CTA is an international tax specialist. He is a Chartered Accountant and Chartered Tax Adviser and is the Editor of the popular tax planning website:

www.wealthprotectionreport.co.uk

Lee is also the author of a number of best selling tax planning books.

OTHER TAX GUIDES

- **Tax Planning Techniques Of The Rich & Famous** - Essential reading for anyone who wants to use the same tax planning techniques as the most successful Entrepreneurs, large corporations and celebrities

- **The Worlds Best Tax Havens 2014/2015** – 220 page book looking at the worlds best offshore jurisdictions in detail

- **Non Resident & Offshore Tax Planning 2014/2015** – Offshore tax planning for UK residents or anyone looking to purchase UK property or trade in the UK. A comprehensive guide.

- **Tax Planning With Offshore Companies & Trusts: The A-Z Guide** - Detailed analysis of when and how you can use offshore companies and trusts to reduce your UK taxes

- **Tax Planning For Company Owners 2014/2015** – How company owners can reduce income tax, corporation tax and NICs

- **How To Avoid CGT In 2013/2014** – Tax planning for anyone looking to reduce UK capital gains tax

- **Buy To Let Tax Planning** – How property investors can reduce income tax, CGT and inheritance tax

- **Asset Protection Handbook** – Looks at strategies to ringfence your assets in today's increasing litigious climate

- **Working Overseas Guide** – Comprehensive analysis of how you can save tax when working overseas

- **Double Tax Treaty Planning** – How you can use double tax treaties to reduce UK taxes

CPSIA information can be obtained at www.ICGtesting.com
Printed in the USA
LVOW10s1835100315

429965LV00036B/1724/P

9 781495 916